Withdrawn from collection

SAN RAFAEL PUBLIC LIBRARY
SAN RAFAEL, CALIFORNIA

P9-EEN-871

DATE DUE

JAN 3 0 1997	
FEB 1 5 1997	
FEB 2 7 1997	
MAR 2 2 1997	
APR 1 2 1997	
MAY 1 6 1997	
JUN 0 6 1997 1997 DEC 1997	
JUN 1 0 1998	
JAN 0 4 1999 MAR − 5 2005 2005 (1)	

GAYLORD   PRINTED IN U.S.A.

San Rafael Public Library
1100 E Street
San Rafael, CA 94901

THE
NEOCLASSICAL
SOURCE BOOK

THE NEOCLASSICAL SOURCE BOOK

CAROLINE CLIFTON-MOGG

RIZZOLI
NEW YORK

San Rafael Public Library
1100 E Street
San Rafael, CA 94901

First published in the United States of America in 1991 by RIZZOLI
INTERNATIONAL PUBLICATIONS, INC.
300 Park Avenue South, New York, NY 10010

Text copyright © 1991 Caroline Clifton-Mogg
Volume copyright © 1991 Cassell, London

All rights reserved
No part of this publication may be reproduced in any manner
whatsoever without prior permission in writing from Rizzoli International
Publications, Inc.

Library of Congress Cataloging-in-Publication Data
Clifton-Mogg, Caroline.
   The neoclassical source book/Caroline Clifton-Mogg.
      p.   cm.
   Includes bibliographical references.
   ISBN 0-8478-1392-4
   1. Neoclassicism (Art)   2. Art, Modern—17th—18th centuries.
I. Title.
N6425.N4C55   1991   91-1124
709′.03′3—dc20   CIP

Printed and bound in Italy

Frontispiece: *The Painted Room in Spencer House, London. Designed and painted 'in
the Antique manner' by James 'Athenian' Stuart between 1759 and 1765, this can claim
to be the earliest complete Neoclassical interior in Europe. The motifs, celebrating the
Triumph of Love, were based closely on Greek and Roman originals.*

CONTENTS

ACKNOWLEDGEMENTS

I would like to thank in general my publishers, Cassell, and in particular Chris Fagg for suggesting that I write this book in the first place. It is necessary also to thank the latter for his soothing encouragement and abiding cheerfulness during the sometimes attenuated process of composition. Stephen Adamson was the most patient and polite editor I have ever worked with, and Christine Wood the most accommodating designer.

My father, Alan Clifton-Mogg, helped me considerably with research; Meredith Etherington-Smith gave many suggestions, and much help and encouragement, as did Selina Hastings. To all three I am very grateful, also to William Drummond, who lightly shared his encyclopedic knowledge with me.

Naturally, I would like to thank my patient husband, Charles Levison, and my tolerant daughters, Eliza and Georgia. I would also like to thank Horace Walpole, Caroline Lybbe Powys and Mrs Delaney for giving me so much lasting pleasure.

Finally, we are grateful to the following for supplying the photographs on the pages listed. Richard Bryant: 193;/Arcaid: 107 (below); David Churchill/Arcaid: 194; Mark Fiennes/Arcaid: 195 (below); Architectural Association: 101, 192; James Austin: 52, 55, 57 (below), 58, 185; Bank of England: 66; Oliver Benn: 74, 75, 76 (×2), 77, 78, 79, 103 (×3), 108, 146, 187 (above), 191; Prof. J. Blankoff: 102 (×2); Bridgeman Archive: 10, 25, 28, 30, 33, 35, 36, 40, 43 (below), 44 (left), 49, 64, 81, 93, 110, 112, 113 (×2), 117, 123 (×2), 124, 125, 129 (×2), 131, 135, 136, 137, 139, 143 (×2), 144 (left), 145, 149 (above), 154, 155 (right), 156, 160 (left), 161, 162 (×2), 163, 164 (×2) 165 (above), 167, 169 (×2), 170, 171, 175, 176,/John Bethel: 68, 96, 97, 116, 119, 120, 121, 122, 179, 182,/Giraudon: 38; Edifice/Darley: 57 (above), 67, 195 (above left),/Drury: 148 (left), 186 (×2); E.T. Archive: 15, 19, 26, 27, 42, 61, 63, 67, 71, 98, 109, 140, 141, 144 (right), 152, 184, 188; E.W.A: 199; Michael Freeman: 31, 32, 84, (below), 85, 91, 106 (below), 149 (below), 151; Garden Picture Library: 187 (below); David George: 9, 82, 104 (×2), 148 (right); John Hall: 159; Angelo Hornak: 12, 22, 44 (right), 45, 46, 51, 53, 56, 59, 69, 70, 85, 92, 105, 107 (above), 127, 130, 147, 150, 155 (left), 158 (×2), 160 (right), 161, 165 (below), 166, 168 (×3), 177, 178, 180, 195 (above right); London Borough of Lambeth Libraries: 115, 134; Lucinda Lambton: frontispiece; Mansell Collection: 13, 14, (×2), 16, 17, 18, 20, 21, 23, 34, 37, 43 (above), 73, 80 (below), 88, 89, 100, 112, 141, 158; David Morrison: 72; National Trust: 126, 138; Hugh Palmer: 181; Fritz von Schulenberg: 62, 198; Sir John Soane's Museum: 50, 133; Edward Teitelman: 80 (above), 83, 84 (above), 86, 95, 106, 174, 190, 197; Andy Williams: 86, 94, 99, 172.

The Farringdon Collection Trust kindly gave permission to reproduce the *couche* by Thomas Hope on p. 165 and the Birmingham Museum and Art Gallery the painting by Claude Lorraine on page 176.

INTRODUCTION

For nearly a hundred years a movement held sway over the arts of the western world to which artists and designers subscribed almost with a moral passion.

Neoclassicism was never a manufactured mode, a fleeting style a grouping of close-cropped and disparate ephemera, nor a label invented for the convenience of art historians. It was the culture of an age when men very deliberately set out to rediscover the virtues of classical art and architecture, and did so in a manner whose results are still relevant today.

The Neoclassical Sourcebook is intended to be an introduction to and celebration of the nature, the pleasure, the varied beauty of Neoclassical design in its key aspects—in particular the architecture and the wide-ranging decorative arts of the period.

One modern dictionary definition of classical is 'of the first rank, and of acknowledged excellence'; a second definition gives 'conforming to the rules of Greek and Latin antiquity'. The doctrine or practice, and together, prefix and adjective conjure up a definitive period of history, when the ideals and ideas of the Ancients were taken as providing rules for architecture, art, and indeed living.

For most people then and now, classical architecture cannot be divorced from the perceived attendant virtues of order and discipline, and it was as much these qualities as the beauty of the forms that have appealed to those who have, through the centuries, led classical revivals. The Neoclassical movement was no exception.

Seen in part as a reaction to the excesses of both the late baroque and rococo styles of architecture, Neoclassicism can effectively be seen to have begun in England in the early eighteenth century with the designs of the Palladians, a group led by the third Earl of Burlington, who designed buildings following the villa designs of the Renaissance architect Andrea Palladio. Its final manifestation was over a century later, epitomized by the buildings of the Greek Revival movement—designs based on thorough and wide-ranging archaeological and academic research.

What Neoclassical design was not was a mere pastiche of columns and capitals, pediments and Palladio. It really was an all-embracing movement, which lent itself not only to the grand designs of architects, but also provided the artistic inspiration of furniture-makers, fabric-designers, jewellers, plasterers and cabinetmakers. From each of these different disciplines came something that was completely new, and yet which was classically inspired.

The main Neoclassical period, during the eighteenth and nineteenth centuries, covered all the arts, including music, as well as architecture and design. It was not simply an artistic and architectural movement, however—although that would be important enough—but a set of ideals that coloured everything from politics to family life. This even accommodated, and was for a time driven by, the revolutionary fervour that was evident in many countries in this period, paramount, of course, in France, and which was sharpened by these images of Neoclassical art and architecture.

Because it was wide in concept, it could, over the years, vary in its identifying characteristics according to the country of origin. In England it became the restrained Regency, in France the monumental Empire, in Germany the provincial Biedermeier, in Scandinavia the airy Gustavian, and in the new United States of America it emerged as the simple Federal style. National signatures were different too—here, heavier, there simpler; gilding and ornament in that corner, marquetry and inlay in the other. But all based the designs, in some way, on the perceived art of Ancient peoples—Egyptians, Greeks and Romans.

Neoclassicism even brought together those who would otherwise seem to have little in common, like Goethe and Robert Adam: although very different artists, they shared a love for the glories of Ancient Rome.

Architecturally, the movement was diverse and far flung, with disciples of all nationalities—many of whom had spent time travelling or working in Italy and Greece—carrying their ideas and designs all round the civilized world, north and east, via Edinburgh to St Petersburg, and west to Virginia and Washington. And it is little wonder there was so much variance within the style, with principal characters as different as the conventional William Chambers, the revolutionary Etienne-Louis Boullée, the visionary John Soane, and the political Thomas Jefferson, all working within the same wide Neoclassical field.

Classical values did not, of course, just spring upon an unsuspecting world, at some unspecified time in the middle of the eighteenth century. Since the beginnings of the Renaissance in the fourteenth century, men, particularly in Europe, had been inspired by what they could see of earlier, ancient civilizations, and artists—Raphael's work at the Villa Madama is a prime example—interpreted Roman ornament in their decorative painting. The work of the Ancient Roman architect, Vitruvius, who wrote between 46 and 30 B.C., had been rediscovered in the early fifteenth century, and was soon reprinted in several languages. But it was the new explosion of interest engendered by the exciting Italian excavations in the towns of both Herculaneum and Pompeii that brought the marvels of the Antique Mediterranean to a new, wider audience, and hastened the flood of the curious to Rome to see the monuments and the art for themselves.

From the first enthusiastic renditions of Palladio's Renaissance villas to the monumental Greek Revival buildings of nearly a century later, not to mention the passing fashions and crazes like the 'goût grec' which swept Paris, and the rash of fashionable rooms painted to imitate the interiors of Pompeii, the classical influence endured long, and continued to exercise its sway well after other styles had come into fashion.

Although, during the early years of the Neoclassical movement, specialized knowledge about the Ancients was a trifle hazy, there was a general approval of the excellence of Ancient architecture. The mathematical care and precision that produced such architectural disciplines as the correct use of the orders, was well appreciated and understood.

It has sometimes seemed, this century, that classicism has been underrated—seen as less important perhaps than the rolling grandeur of the baroque. But today, the classical disicpline is once again seen for what it is—not just an assortment of Greek key motifs, acanthus leaves, and sphinxes' heads, used in predictable and motley fashion, but a manner of architecture, design and decoration that is ageless, and just as applicable to twentieth-century design as it was to the eighteenth century.

Today's architects and designers who use classical forms in their architecture are in many ways going back to the disciplined order and harmony of the classical age. Post-modernists, new classicists, even those who abjure such labels, can all find elements that appeal and are applicable. Classical style is as relevant today as it was two hundred years ago; the river of classicisism runs deep and wide and it is no coincidence that in many countries—not just in Britain, France and the USA—classical design is enjoying a well-deserved renaissance.

The eighteenth-century marbled dining room at Sturehov, near Stockholm, with its fine examples of trompe-l'oeil, *and neoclassical decorative motifs.*

I

THE AGE OF
NEOCLASSICISM

A Roman noblewoman playing the cithara, an elaborate form of the lyre, and seated on a decorated and painted chair, from an excavated fresco.

THE NEOCLASSICAL MOVEMENT IN THE eighteenth and early nineteenth centuries embraced many disciplines, from furniture and architecture to jewellery and ceramics. From Versailles to Virginia, St Petersburg to Edinburgh, ideas were disseminated that were new, original and, most importantly, acceptable to a wide range of society.

There was at that time a desire, strongest perhaps in England and in France, to turn away from what was seen as the ephemera of life, and to turn towards a more truthful vision. In France, it was seen as a wish to return to the values of the Grand Siècle, the reign of Louis XIV, popularly viewed as a time of stability and glory, an era that was characterized in part by its reaction to what had come to be seen as the vapidity of the rococo.

The Antique past, as more became known about it, seemed to hold the key for these enlightened men and women, whose true and moral values were thought of as having been present in Antiquity. The whole Neoclassical identification with the worlds of Ancient Greece and Rome had as much to do with the eighteenth-century perception of early democracy as it did with Antique rules on architecture and design.

The movement grew and spread outwards through Europe, and to Russia and America, over a period of about a hundred years. By the middle of the nineteenth century the style not only extended over architecture and the applied arts—including interior decoration, artefacts and furniture—but also cut a wide swathe through the fine arts of drawing, painting, writing and sculpture, as well as touching upon both philosophy and politics and the non-representational arts like music.

THE GLORIES OF ANCIENT GREECE

The Ancient Greeks believed in harmony, and it was important to them that their architecture reflect this harmony. Religion, too, was all-important. It affected every part of the Greeks' daily lives, and they raised temples to honour their deities. From the early Hellenic period to the later time of Pericles and the building of the Parthenon, some of the most beautiful buildings the world has ever seen were constructed. Over the centuries, the Parthenon itself, the very symbol of Greek design, has been the inspiration for more structures—from churches to conservatories—than any other building ever.

But it was not only architecture at which the Greeks excelled. In each democratic state of Ancient Greece, the artist and writer had the right to pursue free expression in his or her work, and many of the results were artistic masterpieces.

The military and political supremacy of Greece, however, could not last forever: in 146 BC, its energy dissipated and its power weakened, Greece was conquered by Rome, and became one of its provinces.

THE RISE AND FALL OF THE ROMAN EMPIRE

The Romans took, both physically and mentally, all that Greece had to offer—its architecture, its art, its artists—and incorporated all this substance, knowledge and talent into their own culture. Then, true to their role as avid colonizers, they exported these new standards of beauty and excellence all over their rapidly expanding world.

The Romans recognized at once the excellence of what they had found in Greece, for architecture was of great importance to the conquerors. Also Greek sculptures were liberally imported and copied by the Romans, and Hellenic artists and craftsmen, too, began to work in Rome and other parts of the Roman Empire, thus disseminating even further the precepts of classical architecture.

The Romans led both their religious and secular lives very much in public. Their triumphs and victories were public, too, and publicly recorded. Their orators and their statesmen needed splendid backgrounds from which to declaim and impress, and Roman buildings accordingly reflected this extrovert face.

But they did not expend all this creative energy solely on their public buildings. Rich Romans, both in the cities and the country, spent much time planning the design of their own houses—where they should be built, the arrangement of the rooms, and so on. The letters of Pliny the younger

Right: *Piranesi's* Veduto di Campo Vaccino *in Rome, showing various Roman monuments such as the Temple of Concorde, with the Colosseum in the distance. All is depicted in his strong and dramatic manner.*

The roofless interior of the Temple of Diana at Nîmes, one of four vaulted Roman temples built in Europe. Built in the first century BC, the alcoves would originally have held statues of gods or emperors.

(AD 62–113) are much taken up with either descriptions of one of his many houses, or advice to others on architectural details that should be included in their own residences. As far as civic statues went, the practical and politically volatile Romans, knowing that many of their honoured dignitaries would be of short-lived fame, constructed many of their more pedestrian statues with detachable heads, so that a citizen out of favour could simply have his head replaced with that of a more favoured son.

RENAISSANCE INTEREST IN THE ANTIQUE PAST

After the collapse of the Roman Empire, knowledge of classical art, buildings and literature never vanished entirely, but it was not until the late Middle Ages in Italy that there was sufficient prosperity and stability for a widespread resurgence of interest in the arts of the classical world.

Certain famous statues, for instance, were avidly vied for by collectors. The centre of civilized Italy was Florence, and there families like the Medicis were building magnificently decorated houses in which to keep their collections of books and works of art. Greek and Roman classical texts were discovered by a new and wider audience, and cultured men like Pope Nicholas V, who had read many of the newly found classical authors, paid scholars to translate Greek writings into Latin, so that they would be read by all.

Rome itself was mostly a run-down city, with ruined buildings surrounded by the remains of a wall. But the new interest in the arts and the ever-increasing strength of the Popes, who were determined to make

13

Andrea Palladio, born in 1508. His architecture and books, particularly I Quattri Libri dell'Architettura wielded, considerable influence over early neoclassical architecture two centuries after his lifetime.

which were so named because they were located in underground grottoes).

Interested Italians, too, began to make the journey to Rome to see the monuments for themselves. Andrea Palladio (see p.88), for example, was brought to Rome in 1545 by his patron, Giangiorgio Trissino, an experience which influenced him and, through him and his published plans and books, other architects the world over for the next three hundred years.

EXCAVATIONS AND THE BUILDING OF GREAT ART COLLECTIONS

But for all this early academic interest in classical architecture, the princes of the Renaissance themselves generally were not very interested in the crumbling, weed-covered remains of the stone and marble buildings surrounding them. Prints of the time depict the ruins of Rome—not as we see them now, mighty in their fallen grandeur, but instead as earth-covered mounds, with walls and doorways sprouting grass and even trees. It was very difficult for any but those with the most vivid of imaginations to recall the glory that once was Rome. These visionaries took up some of the old ideas—for instance, incorporating columns and capitals into new Renaissance buildings, and even, quite practically, making use of the ready supply of building materials lying all around—but, on the whole, any excavation was sporadic, undertaken either because the land was needed

Rome the powerful centre of a Christian world, encouraged building work to begin. Projects like the building of the Vatican Loggias for Pope Nicholas V (and their decoration under Julius II) were undertaken by artists like the young Raphael, who designed the Loggias and incorporated into them as decoration *grotteschi*, which were copied from paintings found in the recently discovered Domus Aurea, or Golden House of Nero (and

Deathheads, skulls, rams heads, and broken columns by Piranesi. Like many of his contemporaries Piranesi was attracted by the romantic force of ruins.

to build on or in order to find more treasures for nascent art collections.

For it was the art—the sculptures and the paintings—which were then recognized as being of true worth and the principles of architecture, not the ruined buildings themselves. The great Renaissance families of Rome and elsewhere started to build up vast collections, employing excavators to search through the unknown remains. By the beginning of the seventeenth century, the collections of Ancient sculpture amassed by such aristocratic families—particularly those of Popes, like the Medici, Farnese and Borghese—were famous throughout Europe.

HERCULANEUM AND POMPEII

But none of the previous excavations were to have the impact of those begun in 1738 by Charles de Bourbon around the city of Herculaneum, which had been discovered 1719. Of course, his aim was not to find buildings, but, with his museum ever in mind, to unearth additional works of art.

Herculaneum had been destroyed in AD 79, by the same eruption of Vesuvius that had destroyed Pompeii. Unlike Pompeii, however, which

was covered in a layer of relatively soft lapilli and ashes of the sort shrouding the southern slopes of Vesuvius, Herculaneum, farther away in the path of the eruption, was covered by a river of flowing lavic material. The lava was turned into a sea of mud by the accompanying torrential rains, and eventually it hardened into a stonelike material—in essence, a near-impenetrable coffin, over twelve metres high, that engulfed the entire city.

These first excavations into Herculaneum were carried out by entering through well openings. These were then used as mine shafts through which, after tunnelling farther through the hard core, paintings, sculptures and other works of art could be retrieved. Then, astonishingly, around 1740 the excavations were filled in, and there was very little documentation to show what had been done—and what had been discovered. Digging resumed, however, in 1745. The works went slowly (some years were totally void of excavation), but generally continued until 1765, by which time many foreign archaeologists and historians were involved. Then the site was sealed again, not to be reopened until 1828.

Pompeii, under its layer of ash and lava, was easier to excavate. Work here began in 1748 and continued without interruption well into the next

The Colosseum in Rome, painted in 1846 by Lipot Kelpel. The grandeur of classical decay exercised a spell on several generations of painters.

century, revealing not only treasures and well-preserved buildings, but also a wealth of information about how the Romans had lived and worked. Indeed, the passion for excavation, once started, lasted a long time. From the 1700s right up to the middle of the nineteenth century, new things were constantly being discovered, and even in our own time, digs still continue at both Pompeii and Herculaneum.

THE BUYING AND SELLING OF RENAISSANCE COLLECTIONS

The impressive Renaissance collections of classical art soon came on the market, the buyers either other Italian families or rich, often royal families from other European countries. However, it was difficult for outsiders, no matter how exalted, to purchase the originals. Certainly it was not possible simply to arrive in the city, find a small piece of Antique Rome and leave with it packed into a valise. By the eighteenth century, excavations were regulated by law in the Papal States, and the export of works of art was subjected to controls. All sales of antiquities were under the control of the Commissioner of Antiquities. Most foreign collectors had to be content with either bronze or plaster casts of the most significant sculptures; in that

form the images travelled far across the civilized world.

By the first decade of the eighteenth century, the first Italian collectors had begun the dispersal of some of their artworks, and interested English, French, Spanish and other parties either started or added to their collections. Don Livio Odelaschi, nephew of Pope Innocent XI, had obtained his treasures in the first place in 1692 from one of the great early collectors, Queen Christina of Sweden, and in 1724 they were to sold King Philip V of Spain. The Chigi family sold some antiquities to the Elector of Saxony in 1728, and five years later Cardinal Alessandro Albani, one of the most knowledgeable of collectors, sold his works to Pope Clement XII, who created a new museum, the Capitoline, around them.

THE GROWTH OF COLLECTING

There had long been some English specialist collectors, notably the Earl of Arundel, who during the 1600s both went in search of treasures himself and employed other people to find him pieces—and their journeys were not limited to Italy. Although Greece was not generally considered a source of antiquities until two centuries later, by 1620 there were already a few prospective antiquities seekers there. One such emissary was Lord

Left: *Early eighteenth-century excavations at Herculaneum, the ancient town on the sea that had been swamped by Vesuvius. The hard outer layers of mud and tufa made exploration slow and laborious.*

Eighteenth-century English view of the Temple of Isis at Pompeii, whose high walls hid from public view the sacred mysteries within. It stood on a tall podium with an atrium of six columns—four in the front, and two at either side.

Arundel's chaplain, Mr Petty, of whom Sir Thomas Roe—who was doing the same sort of work for the Duke of Buckingham—said: 'He encounters all accidents with unwearied patience, eats with Greeks on their workdays; lies with fishermen on planks, is all things that may obtain his ends.' Such devotion paid off, for the collection later known as the Arundel Marbles was large and varied.

The advent of the Civil War, however, and the earl's death during it, marked the end of the Arundel collection as such. After its dispersal parts of it would form the nuclei of several other collections that were to become famous: those of Lord Pembroke at Wilton, the Duke of Devonshire, Lord Burlington and Thomas Coke, later Earl of Leicester.

These early indications of the treasures of Greece notwithstanding, on the whole Italy was better known and exploited by the treasure-seeking English. Nobles like Lords Burlington and Leicester began to commission other Englishmen already based in Rome to excavate on site, and to send back whatever antiquities they found.

Gavin Hamilton (1723–98), a Scottish history painter, arrived in Rome in 1748 and was later one of these amateur excavators. In the 1760s, he acted as archaeologist for Charles Towneley among others, in 1770 undertaking more excavations at Hadrian's Villa, where several fine sculptures had already been found. He and Towneley corresponded regularly about possible new sites, and the pieces he found were sent to England through an agent, Thomas Jenkins.

By 1770, excavations were taking place all around the Eternal City. The Lateran was excavated in 1779–80, and the Villa dei Quintilii was found on the Appian Way between 1783 and 1785. At all these sites both important and minor works were found. Nowhere were sculptures, and statues in particular, in short supply, for in the decadent days of the late Roman Empire every newly wealthy citizen wanted his own statue. At the time the historian Ammianus Marcellinus wrote, rather disapprovingly, about the need for these nouveau riche to not only have their own statue—often in bronze—but to have it gilded as well. Their vanity was to be a boon for the noblemen of a later civilization.

Despite the fact that sculptures were not in short supply at the height of this 'archaeological boom,' there was a certain amount of faking, or at least of wishful thinking, going on. Where once a face might have had a new nose modelled to replace one that was lost, by the height of the boom armless torsos were being refitted with new limbs made to satisfy an approximate rather than a correct position. This had been happening since the first collections were being formed in the sixteenth century, and by the eighteenth century there were several restorers working in Rome who could turn their hands to this slightly more creative form of 'reconstruction.' But as the collectors became more knowledgeable, they returned these dubious pieces. Records show that Charles Towneley sent back several pieces back to Thomas Jenkins a few years after he had received them.

THE GRAND TOUR

By 1700, it was quite usual for young European men of good birth to undertake the Grand Tour. The journey encompassed various Continental sites: the wonders of France and the richness and pomp of the French court, the splendours of the papal court and those of noble Roman and Florentine families. The tour was usually made with an educated companion, often a young architect or painter. The English seem to have been thought of as the best tutors and guides for the trip—even the young Goethe dreamed of being accompanied to Italy by an educated Englishman, 'well versed in general history and history of art'. Some even settled in Rome and became permanent tourist guides, often doing a little dealing in antiquities on the side.

Italy became increasingly important on the Grand Tour, as more splendid collections came on view and more sites had excavators sifting through their ruins. Paintings and sculptures (both originals and casts) were bought, shipped back to England and viewed with wonder by all. Some, however, were shocked by the condition of the monuments. Horace Walpole, who was there in 1739, wrote: 'By the remains one sees of the Roman grandeur in these structures, it is evident that there must have been more pains taken to destroy those piles than to raise them. They are more demolished than any time or chance could have affected.'

But shocking or not, the possible scope of the excavations, and the sight of the treasures and civilization that had already emerged, led to an explosion of interest in the outside world. Men from civilized countries everywhere were fascinated by the idea of this lost world—these monuments to past great empires—and began to arrive in Rome in their hundreds. It is hard to imagine now what impact the buried drama of Italy and Greece must have held for those educated travellers, who had read so much and travelled so far to view the remains. Goethe, not known for his outbreaks of passion, said on arriving in Rome in November 1786:

Now, at last, I have arrived in the First City of the world! ... Now that I have arrived, I have calmed down and feel as if I had found a peace that will last for my whole life. Because, if I may say so, as soon as one sees with one's own eyes the whole which one had hitherto only known in fragments ... a new life begins.

All the dreams of my youth have come to life; the first engravings I remember—my father hung views of Rome in the hall—I now see in reality, and everything I have known for so long through paintings, drawings, etchings, woodcuts, plaster casts and cork models is now assembled before me. Wherever I walk, I come upon familiar objects in an unfamiliar world; everything is just as I imagined it, yet everything is new.

J. W. Goethe, painted in 1787 by his friend and countryman Johann Heinrich Wilhelm Tischbein. Painted whilst they were both in Rome, Goethe is depicted as a traveller, sitting on a fallen obelisk and looking towards the ruins of the Campagna di Roma. He himself said that 'the likeness was striking'.

Left: *Piranesi's view of the temple of Cibele, in the Piazza della Bocca della Verità. The building looks as if it has become a wheelwright's storeroom, but this did not prevent Piranesi finding the portico 'very noble'.*

The remains of the Great Temple of the Sun at Palmyra which with its giant Corinthian column once dominated the city. It was first described and drawn by Wood and Dawkins, on a journey financed by the Society of Dilettanti.

force behind many of the important eighteenth-century publications that led the field in collecting and disseminating information was an unlikely-sounding gentlemen's dining club, the Society of Dilettanti, founded by, among others, the infamous Sir Francis Dashwood, a known reprobate and rake. Established in England in 1734 as a sociable dining society, the club originally comprised a group of about forty young noblemen and gentlemen, all of whom were veterans of the Grand Tour. Over the next twenty years, the society developed into a body of like-minded men whose aim was to act as patrons to architects and archaeologists, to further knowledge of the Antique world, and to commission and finance exploratory expeditions, afterwards paying to produce folios or papers on the discoveries made.

The toast of the Society of Dilettanti was 'To Grecian taste and Roman Spirit', their president wore a toga to preside at meetings and their membership included noted collectors, politicians and artists. Earl Harcourt, Earl Temple, and the Dukes of Devonshire and Dorset all belonged to the society, as did Sir James Gray, who, when envoy to Naples, organized a subscription in Venice for a proposed work on Athens that architect-painters James Stuart (1713–88) and Nicholas Revett (1720–1804) were planning, and later took a prominent part in the excavations at Herculaneum. In a country without a body like the Académie Française, the Society of Dilettanti deserves much credit for instigating much initial work, both immediate and long-lasting, on Ancient archaeological sites, and in particular for encouraging the exploration and excavation of both the well-known Roman and less familiar Greek sites.

By this time, the road to Rome was relatively well trodden, and easy to get to for those who wished to record the monuments, but Greece and the other sites of Greek remains in Asia Minor were still considered inaccessible. Few had seen the temples of Athens, although in 1674 the Marquis de Nointel, then French Ambassador to the Ottoman Porte, was instructed by Colbert to visit Athens and record what he saw. With the help of two artists, Rombaut Faydherbe and Jacques Carrey, he drew in chalk the remains of the sculptures that had once decorated the Parthenon. They were not in good condition even then—the Turks, currently occupying Athens, had neglected them badly—but at least a record was made, nearly a century before others were to see them.

EARLY PUBLICATIONS ON ANTIQUITIES

There are few mentions of other records of Ancient art, so the stir that was caused in 1753 by one of the earliest publications funded by the Society of Dilettanti was enormous. This was *The Ruins of Palmyra*, followed by *The Ruins of Baalbec* in 1757, both produced by James Dawkins and Robert Wood after an expedition to Asia Minor between 1750 and 1753. Earlier in conception, but later in publication, Stuart and Revett's *The Antiquities of Athens* was also to have long-lasting influence.

Stuart and Revett arrived in Rome in 1742, staying on for some years to draw and measure the ruins there. Their subsequent plan was to record the then little-known ruins of Athens, and in 1750 they quit Rome and went to Venice, where they met up with Sir James Gray. They reached Athens in 1751, and remained until 1753, but were unable to finish their work there because of the disturbances in Athens after the death of the Ottoman

The Pont du Gard at Nîmes, part of a 40-kilometre (25 miles) long aqueduct built by the Romans in 1 BC as part of a European network of aqueducts.
Comprising three tiers of arches, the bridge crossed the valley 60 metres (180 ft) above the ground.

Sultan Osma. Thus, it was some time after returning home before they were able to publish their work, during which time the Frenchman J.-D. Le Roy, after a trip to Athens in 1753—and well aware of the Englishmen's delay—published his own work, *Les Ruines des plus beaux monuments de la Grèce* in 1758, beating Stuart and Revett by four years.

In 1764, the first expedition to Ionia—encompassing parts of what is now Turkey—took place. Dr Richard Chandler, his assistant Nicholas Revett and artist William Pars went from England to Smyrna—present-day Izmir—and from there to ancient sites like Miletus and Priene, returning eventually to Athens. The first volume of the much-acclaimed fruit of their expedition, *Antiquities of Ionia*, was published by the Society of Dilettanti in London in 1769.

There was a great deal of competitiveness among these early 'explorer-authors' to travel to, document and then publish notes on and images of historic sites, one reason being that books on Ancient architecture, whether Greek or Roman, were both extremely popular and highly prestigious for writer and publisher alike. Without the benefits of twentieth-century communication, these published folios of drawings, descriptions and measurements of Antique architecture had enormous influence—many of them for several generations. As well as being of historical value, they provided plans and ideas on which the new class of landowners could base their houses.

Another factor that added to an increase of knowledge about the Ancient world was the publication of English historian Edward Gibbon's *The History of the Decline and Fall of the Roman Empire* (1776–88). An immediate bestseller, the multipart history made Gibbon famous, and placed the unsettled and insecure last years of Imperial Rome into a contemporary context for many an eighteenth-century reader.

THE BRITISH ART COLONY IN ROME

By the early 1700s, there was a fairly large colony of British artists in Rome. They included, among others, the history painter Gavin Hamilton, who, in response to an increasing demand from his homeland, depicted various scenes set against Roman ruins, all intended to be hung on stately British walls. As mentioned earlier, Hamilton later spent much time excavating and restoring antiquities, and his influence at the beginning of the movement loomed large. Another restorer of note was Matthew Brettingham, who, after buying a large number of both sculptures and casts for the Earl of Leicester, later returned to England to work on the Earl's Neoclassical wonder, Holkham Hall in Norfolk.

Some Britons were in Rome by virtue of the Society of Dilettanti, others, like Brettingham, through the good offices of a rich patron who was interested in the arts and architecture and desirous of either having some of the wonders painted by his protégé or even buying some classical work of art. Still others actually hoped to reproduce some of the architectural wonders of Antiquity on their own land in Great Britain.

Such an early patron was Richard Boyle, the 3rd Earl of Burlington (1694–1753), who went to Italy for the first time in 1714 when he was twenty. He admired much that he saw in Italy, indeed all he saw in Rome. While in Italy, he also read some of the works of the sixteenth-century architect, Palladio, which deeply impressed him. On a second visit to Italy several years later, Burlington took in all Palladio's villas in the Veneto, and in 1719 he returned to England with his own protégé, William Kent, determined to spread the gospel of Palladianism throughout Britain. Burlington was very much a man of his time, interested in architecture, painting, archaeology and the other arts, and his influence during the early years of the Neoclassical movement was great.

GREAT ENGLISH COLLECTORS OF THE 1700s

The bases of many fine English collections were formed in the mid- to late eighteenth century. Among these early amateurs of Antique art were Charles Towneley, Henry Blundell of Ince Blundell Hall and the Marquess of Lansdowne. There was also Thomas Coke, the 1st Earl of Leicester, who built Holkham Hall; William Weddell, known later for the Weddell Marbles at his seat, Newby Hall; Charles Wyndham, the 2nd Earl of Egremont at Petworth House; and the Duke of Bedford at Woburn Abbey. At the beginning of the nineteenth century came Lord Elgin, who brought back to England pieces of the Parthenon, and Thomas Hope, who, on the death of Sir William Hamilton, bought the second collection Hamilton had amassed. Hope and most of the above were members of the Society of Dilettanti.

Thomas Howard, second Earl of Arundel, painted by Paul van Somer (c. 1577-1622) and pictured in Arundel castle with part of his famous collection of antiquities. Arundel was among the earliest of classical collectors; after his death the collection was split up and the parts became the bases of several important eighteenth-century collections.

Perhaps more than anyone else, Charles Towneley personified the typical eighteenth-century collector, and he is doubly interesting because much of his collection remains intact, where it can be seen today in the British Museum in London. Rich and knowledgeable, he was also a member of the Society of Dilettanti, living in Rome from 1765 to 1772. He was a friend of Sir William Hamilton (husband of Emma), and promoted Gavin Hamilton (no relation) and Thomas Jenkins in their excavating work in Rome. Returning to London, he built a large house at 7 Park Street, Westminster (now Queen Anne's Gate), which was designed solely to house his collection of antiquities. Gavin Hamilton was employed to search out new works of art for Towneley, and not only did Hamilton excavate but he also did some restoration on the pieces he found before sending them back to London. *Charles Towneley in his Gallery*, the well-known painting by Johann Zoffany (now in the Towneley Hall Museum, Burnley, Lancashire), shows the collector surrounded by his favourite objects at his home in Park Street.

Because there were artists and archaeologists on site in Rome, it is often thought that the works of art arrived in England in near-pristine condition, ready to grace the new galleries designed for them in the homes of noblemen. But contemporary sources reveal that quite often the pieces arrived in a far worse state.

William Hugh Dalton, in *The New and Complete English Traveller*, a leisured look at the houses and places of interest in the counties of England, which was published about 1796, described a visit to Petworth House in Sussex. Charles Wyndham, the late 2nd Earl of Egremont, had amassed a large collection of antiquities:

> The principal apartments are furnished with antique statues and busts, some of which are of the first-rate value; a singular circumstance attending them is, that a great many when the late Earl bought them, were complete invalids; some wanting heads, others hands, feet, noses, etc. These mutilations his lordship endeavoured to supply, by the application of new members, very ill suited either in complexion, or elegance of finishing, to the Roman and Grecian trunks; so that, in some respects, this stately fabric gives us the idea of a large hospital, or receptacle, for wounded and disabled statues.

THE FRENCH AND GERMAN COMMUNITIES IN ROME

The English were not the only architects and painters working in Rome, although they did represent a large proportion of the foreigners. There was also a large community from Germany, and another, of long standing, from France. There was then, as there is today, the French Académie à Rome, where winners of the Académie's Grand Prix de Rome were sent. As *pensionnaires*, they would live and work in Rome for several years, extending their skills and increasing their knowledge of Antiquity. There was also the Accademia de San Luca, whose competitions were eagerly entered by the expatriate students.

One result of this polyglot population was that young men of much the same age and interests met and spent several years in each other's company, building up relationships that were later important in the spread of Neoclassical ideas across the world. The benefits were both practical, as they helped each other with commissions, and intellectual, as they exchanged ideas and thoughts.

Away from Rome, these new ideas were also promulgated in Paris by the influential school set up by J.-F. Blondel in 1743. Many of the future Neoclassical architects were trained there, including the Englishman William Chambers. Similarly, although later, in Berlin there was an equally influential school run by a father and son, David and Friedrich Gilly, where men like Karl Friedrich Schinkel, considered the architect of Neoclassical Berlin, were first trained.

THE PUBLIC DISPLAY OF ANTIQUITIES

In 1772 the new Museo Pio Clementino was opened in the Vatican. There was no more space for the continuing flood of finds in the rooms of the Vatican or the existing Capitoline Museum, and both Clement XIV and Pius VI, his successor, expanded it, anxious that it should reflect the glory of the Popes. This was the beginning of a new concept—an interest in disseminating information through access to the works. Hitherto, the idea of museums had not been much thought of by the educated classes, but now they were seen both as a source of widespread knowledge and, of course, a reflection of the munificence of their founders.

In England, too, art collections were being shown to a wider audience. Charles Lennox, the 3rd Duke of Richmond and a member of the Society of Dilettanti, formed a collection of classical paintings, sculptures and casts at an early age, and in 1760 had a sculpture gallery built in the garden of his house at Whitehall, and had it decorated by William Chambers. He displayed his collection there, where it was also used for study by various artists.

By 1788 London had become the centre of the trade in Ancient art and antiquities, and collectors such as Towneley bought regularly from Christie's.

THE INFLUENCE OF THE ANTIQUE ON FINE ARTISTS

As with other important design movements, it was not just the classical architecture that was important to Neoclassicism. Artists and sculptors, too, came to Rome and then produced their own version of the classical world. Among them were the Frenchman Claude Lorrain, with his pastoral Arcadian landscapes; the German Anton-Raphael Mengs, with his 'history paintings' that purported to show events in a suitable Antique way; and, most influential of all, Jacques-Louis David. Much influenced by his visit to Rome, David then started to paint revolutionary subjects portrayed in classical Antique settings, and to find a form to express political thoughts and views. He managed to suggest, indeed to forge a link between, the ideals of Antiquity and the democratic feeling of pre-revolutionary France. The latter was understood and embraced by much of France, although the French generally took little interest in either the

Charles Towneley in the specially built gallery of his house in London. Painted by Johann Zoffany, he is surrounded by part of his collection of antiquities, including the Venus found at Ostia and the youthful Bacchus. Seen with him are his fellow antiquarians Charles Greville and Sir Thomas Astle.

classical revival or the collecting of antiquities until after the Revolution.

Far from being just a group of different but related buildings, paintings and decorative *objets d'art* that happened to be executed between the mid-1700s and early 1800s in several countries, Neoclassicism fired a part of two generations that was eager to look at their world with new ideas. The original classical revival of the Renaissance had drifted off into mannerism, the baroque and the rococo, and the latter was particularly identified with an *ancien règime* that was running out of ideas. Especially after the American War of Independence, radical social and political ideas

were gaining widespread currency in Europe. An art style was needed to go with this, and it was provided by the same inspiration as David found in the heroes of the Antique world. It was not Imperial Rome that appealed to the new generation, but the Republican Rome that had thrown out the kings, and the ancient Greece of the democratic city state of Athens.

It may have been far from the minds of the aristocratic collectors who first went to Rome with their artistic advisers that this would happen, but the Neoclassical was to be adopted by the increasingly important middle classes, who enjoyed the simplicity and nobility of its forms.

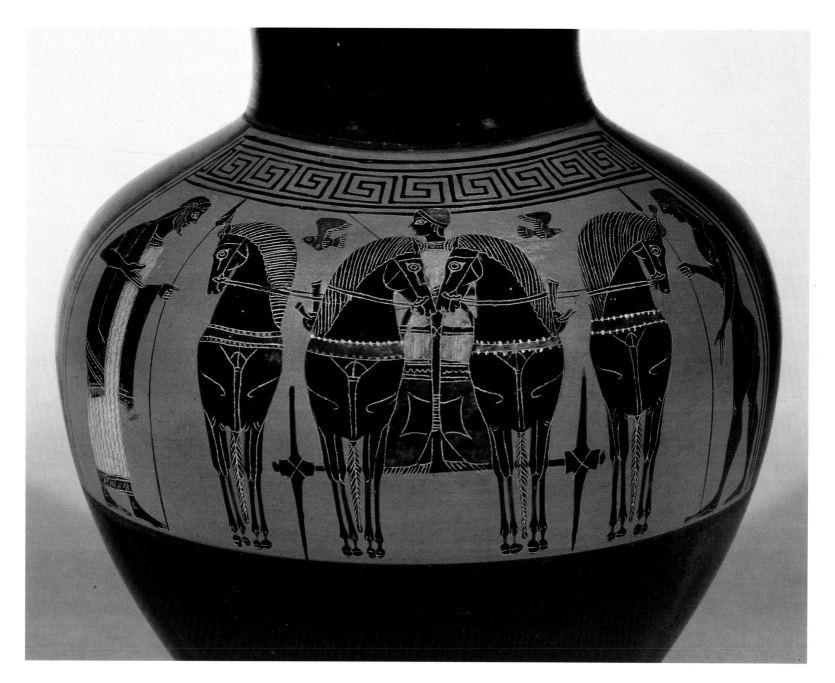

A Greek black figure vase, depicting a charioteer and his horses. Both the shapes of these ancient vessels, and the scene they depicted, were drawn on heavily by Neoclassical craftsmen.

Right: A Greek red amphora of figurines showing a woman playing a flute-type instrument of a type popular in Greek households. Such works were to inspire a whole genre of ceramics.

II

NEOCLASSICAL
ART

I N THE EIGHTEENTH CENTURY, EVERY man of education was a
connoisseur of art, and anyone with breeding, schooling and—more importantly—money, collected paintings and sculpture. For the new aspiring
middle classes, pictures of themselves or others were easier to buy than
houses, and gave them social credibility. Throughout Europe, Italian
Renaissance paintings were avidly bought, as were contemporary French,
Italian and, to a lesser degree, English works. Collecting works of art was
to become a veritable mania.

Everyone who was anyone knew about painting in the eighteenth
century. More than architecture, more than furniture, it was paintings and
painters that exercised the minds of the polite classes. In an age that had
only just devised the concept of the public museum, it was probably not
surprising that the less priviledged wanted to see private paintings. Until
the opening of galleries and museums in cities like London, Berlin,
Munich and Paris, paintings and sculpture remained very much the private
property of their owners, and the owners of great houses therefore had an

Cupid and Psyche, *a sculpture by Antonio Canova. Settling in Rome in 1780,
Canova, who worked mostly with marble but also other materials including terracotta,
based his work, and many of his subjects, on the idea of the Antique ideal. Famous in his
lifetime, he worked on commissions for most of the collectors of his day, including
Napoleon Bonaparte.*

obligation, in the eyes of the public, to allow their paintings to be minutely inspected on visits by interested passers-by.

From Celia Fiennes to Horace Walpole, travellers took note of what they saw. The subjects and compositions were duly noted and remarked upon, and in some cases, as Mrs Delany pointed out, help was given with identification. When the latter visited the cultured Lord Bute's house at Luton in 1774, she noted that 'Every room [was] filled with pictures, many capital ones, and a handsome screen hangs by each fireside, with the plan of the room, and with the names of the hand by whom the pictures were painted, in the order as they stand.'

Both English and French monarchs had collected paintings for decades, but by the middle of the eighteenth century, the French collections were the more spectacular. The paintings were moved around from palace to palace, under the aegis of the Directeur des Bâtiments du Roi. In the 1760s, the Marquis de Marigny, brother of Mme de Pompadour, held this position. The English connoisseur Horace Walpole, staying in Paris in 1765 stated:

> I went to see the reservoir of pictures at Monsieur de Marigny's. They are what are not disposed of in the palaces, though sometimes changed with others. This Refuse, which fills many rooms from top to bottom, is composed of the most glorious works of Raphael, L. da Vinci, Giorgione, Titian, Guido, Corregio etc. Many pictures, which I knew by their prints, without an idea where they existed, I found here.

PRINTS AND PAINTINGS AS CHRONICLES OF THE ANTIQUE

The reference to prints as a source of identification is interesting. As the eighteenth century progressed, printmaking had become more and more general; most major paintings were issued in print form, and by the end of the century the print had become an effective means of mass communication. Whether employed as an artistic tool—as with the reproduction of a new painting—or engraved specially as a means of purveying news or propaganda to make a moral or political point, their popularity was immediate, and remained so for the next hundred years.

Many paintings recorded paintings. Zoffany's picture, *The Tribuna in the Uffizi*, which shows a group of dilettante art lovers admiring works of art in the Florence gallery, was commissioned by Queen Charlotte so that she could see the finest works that the Uffizi had to offer. In the pair of

A Roman capriccio showing the Colosseum, Borghese warrior, Trajan's Column, and the Dying Gaul by Giovanni Paolo Pannini. English gentlemen in the Grand Tour hired the services of a Roman guide (or in some cases an English one) to acquaint them with the monuments of antiquity.

Right: *A bas-relief in heroic mode from the pediment of the State Capitol, Washington DC, a building that was designed, as the result of a competition, by a Frenchman and two Englishmen. Itself inspired by the works of Andrea Palladio, it in turn became the nineteenth-century inspiration for many later public buildings, particularly in America.*

paintings executed by Gian Paolo Panini in 1757 called *Modern Rome* and *Ancient Rome*—both comprising canvases within frames—the former depicted views of Renaissance and later Rome, the latter vistas of an earlier, Ancient Rome, as it appeared to an eighteenth-century chronicler.

ARTISTS RECORDING THE PAST

Painters, and to a certain extent sculptors, played a very practical role during this time as essential recorders of contemporary life and experiences. Without photography or film, the wonders of the excavations and other sights of the Grand Tour, for example, could only be recorded on paper or canvas. Wealthy nobles, like the Earl of Burlington, took their own painters with them through Europe to record vital moments. Other less-encumbered travellers on arriving in Rome would commission one of the vast pool of painters already resident there to work for them.

In addition to the fledgling architects and young gentlemen of noble birth in Rome in the eighteenth century were a large number of painters and sculptors, all of whom had come to see and learn. Some, mostly French, were there, at the Académie Française at Rome, as award-winning students from the Académie in Paris; others were there by the good offices of rich patrons, and some went to this universal centre under their own steam. Every nationality had a small colony there: the English, the Scots, the French, the Germans, and even the Russians and Americans.

Those artists who paid their own fares often made enough money to support themselves, either by painting particular views for rich men coming to see the sights or some of the grand travellers in front of an imposing Ancient monument in order to prove to posterity that they had been there. Nobles flocked to painters like Pompeo Battoni (1708–87) to be captured in suitably sophisticated pose against some identifiable great Antique work.

GREAT AND LESSER ANTIQUE STATUARY

The Antique sculptures accepted by people of taste and education as representing the pinnacle of artistic achievement were possibly even more famous then than they are now, and were recognized everywhere. The Laocoon, the Belvedere Apollo, the Farnese Hercules and the Venus de'Medici—to take four of the best known—were copied in every medium possible. In the 1981 book, *Taste and the Antique*, Francis Haskell and Nicholas Penny noted that the Venus de'Medici was copied for the Duke of Marlborough in bronze; for Louis XIV once in bronze and five times in marble; in lead for innumerable gardens, and in plaster for even more numerous interiors. It was inevitable that these images would influence both artists and sculptors in their work.

A figure of Ludwig I of Bavaria adorning the Walhalla near Regensburg, in Bavaria, designed by Leo von Klenze between 1830 and 1842. This monumental temple, much influenced by the Parthenon, was one of the most obviously Grecian buildings of the German Classical Revival.

THE APPEAL OF HISTORY PAINTINGS

Prominent among this multinational Roman set was Gavin Hamilton, known not only for his excavation and restoration work, but also for his history paintings. He lived in Rome for many years and, as well as being the centre of the English circle—both permanent and peripatetic—he produced large paintings based on scenes or supposed events of Ancient times.

History paintings—that is to say, products of the school of painting that sought to represent historical or indeed mythological events, but usually with a moral point—were much sought after by the mid-eighteenth century. They were considered proper subjects for painters to work on, unlike the flim-flam of the rococo portraits, landscapes and rural idylls. According to Hugh Honour (in his definitive book, *Neoclassicism*), M. Lenormant de Tournehem, the uncle of Mme de Pompadour, decreed in 1745, when he held the post of Directeur des Bâtiments du Roi, that in order to reinstate the correct balance between the serious and frivolous, history painters were to be paid more for their work than artists still working in the rococo style.

The German artist Anton Raphael Mengs (1728–79) was another leading classical history painter. Mengs was a friend and compatriot of the critic Winckelmann, who was working at that time in Rome as the librarian of the great collector and connoisseur, Cardinal Albani. Indeed, Mengs painted *Parnassus* for the central room of Cardinal Albani's villa.

A member of Mengs' circle in Rome was Joseph Marie Vien (1716–1809), who on his return to France after six years in Italy, began to paint 'Greek subjects' inspired by the grace of Greek sculpture, one of the earliest painters in France to do so. Vien trained many later Neoclassical artists, including David and François-Xavier Fabre (1766–1837); Fabre became a well-known Neoclassical portraitist, often depicting other artists—he is particularly known for his portrait of the sculptor Antonio Canova of 1812.

Ossian Receiving the Generals of the Republic, by Anne-Louis Girodet-Trioson, a pupil of David's. The idealized figures in heroic poses were typical of Neoclassical painters, who often included classical references, and garbed their figures in Roman costume. The painting was commissioned by Napoleon in 1802, and intended for the grand salon at Malmaison.

PIRANESI AND WINCKELMANN: ROME VERSUS ATHENS

Any account, however brief, of Neoclassical art and sculpture, has to admit the vital part played by Giovanni Battista Piranesi. Apart from his influence on the young architects who saw the monuments of Ancient Rome through his theatrical eyes, after he settled in Rome in 1744 he used his position to champion the supremacy of Roman art and architecture over that of the Greeks. He mainly lobbied his arguments against the central champion of Greek art, Winckelmann, who had never actually been to Athens. Piranesi's views—mostly etchings that developed in an increasingly dramatic manner, using shadow, light and contorted proportions that stressed the greatness of Rome as it towered above ant-like humans—had an enormous influence on many artists' perceptions and work.

Johann Joachim Winckelmann, Piranesi's adversary, was one of the most thought-provoking and voluble of eighteenth-century artistic theorists. Seeing the Antique as that which should be imitated—in its widest sense—he spent most of his working life proselytizing for the artistic supremacy of Greece over Rome, both in architectural and fine-art terms, particularly sculpture. Many of his arguments and conclusions were based on his experience in his privileged position as librarian to Cardinal Albani.

THE PAINTINGS OF DAVID

Middle-class opinion in France in the years leading up to the French Revolution was, on a simple level, turning away from the excesses of much of the aristocracy, but also, on a deeper level, turning towards a more austere concept of life. The Revolution and the Terror that followed affected art as much as every other area of French life. There was no more room for pleasurable fantasy—realism and patriotic inspiration were required.

Of all the names associated with Neoclassical art, that of Jacques-Louis David (1748–1825) is arguably the best known, and certainly the most influential. He understood the aspirations of the Revolution and felt one with its proponents; he recognized his role to portray those hopes and aims, and to encourage the seeds of revolution and reform.

David trained under Vien, and did not travel to Rome until he was 34, staying for seven years and drinking in all the city's riches. After returning to Paris and then again going to Rome, he painted the work for which he is best known, *The Oath of the Horatii*. Intended as an inspirational picture, the painting portrays the virtues of patriotism and idealism set in the true classical past.

J. J. Winckelmann, the critic who extolled the merits of Greek architecture over Roman—a controversy that ran for many years. The bust stands in the gardens of the Villa Albani in Rome where Winckelmann lived and worked as librarian to the collector Cardinal Albani.

The Oath of the Horatii *by Jaques-Louis David, the painter who was perhaps most identified with the aims and ideals of the French Revolution. With its portrayal of the classical virtues of loyalty and bravery the painting itself was seen as capturing the mood of the times.*

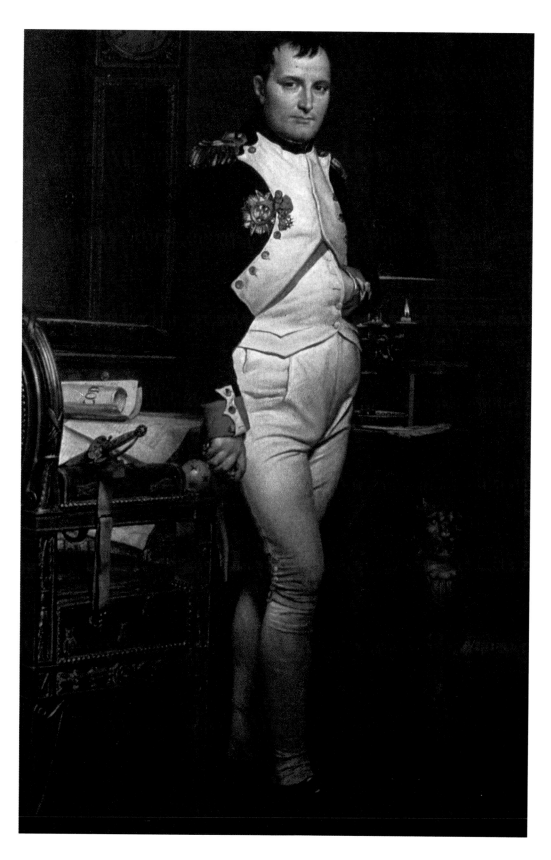

Napoleon in His Study *by David.*
David tries to capture the imposing
stillness of much classical statuary, and
the figure is depicted from a low vantage
point so as to appear dominant.

During the Revolution, David became a deputy in the National Convention. Under his aegis, in an effort to limit the power of academies of painting and sculpture, the directorship of the Académie at Rome was abolished and, finally, in 1793, the academies themselves were suppressed.

David's paintings remained a prime source of propaganda and inspiration upon Napoleon's accession. In the same way that various triumphal monuments—notably the triumphal column in the Place Vendôme that was modelled on Trajan's Column—sought to establish a link between the New Emperor and those of old, so David's portrayal of Napoleon in imperial garb helped his subject's identification with the Emperors of Rome become universally known. Indeed, he made use of classical symbols in all his Imperial commissions. In the set-piece propaganda paintings, heroic gestures and groupings were modelled on the Antique, and in the more intimate portraits, such as *Napoleon in His Study*, furniture ornamented with the distinctive Neoclassical emblems of the Empire was shown in detail. Their role is not mere fashion; it is to reinforce the association with the classical past.

THE SCULPTURE OF CANOVA

Empire-period sculpture, too, expressed the sentiments of the time. Antonio Canova (1757–1822), the Italian sculptor much patronized by the Bonaparte family (as well as its foes), first trained in Venice, then went to Rome in 1780. He was struck there, not by the Antique majesty of the excavated sculptures, but by their expression of contemporary ideals. He became part of the group Gavin Hamilton moved with, a set that combined interests in archaeology, painting and sculpture. Canova's success was immediate; he carved monuments for Popes Clement XIII and XIV that were known and admired throughout Europe, and his talents were in great demand—Catherine the Great in Russia, Francis II in Vienna and Napoleon in Paris all wanted him to work for them. But he preferred to stay in Rome, where his œuvre took on a new strength as he worked, not as an imitator of Antique sculpture, but as a modern artist who tried to work in the same way as his ancestors had, with the same goals of simplicity and idealism. He did not carve marble to express lace collars or satin skirts, as some of the baroque sculptors had done. His aim was to strip away excess ornament to reveal the soul beneath.

Pauline Bonaparte as Venus Vincitrice, *sculpted in marble by Antonio Canova, in typically classical pose.*

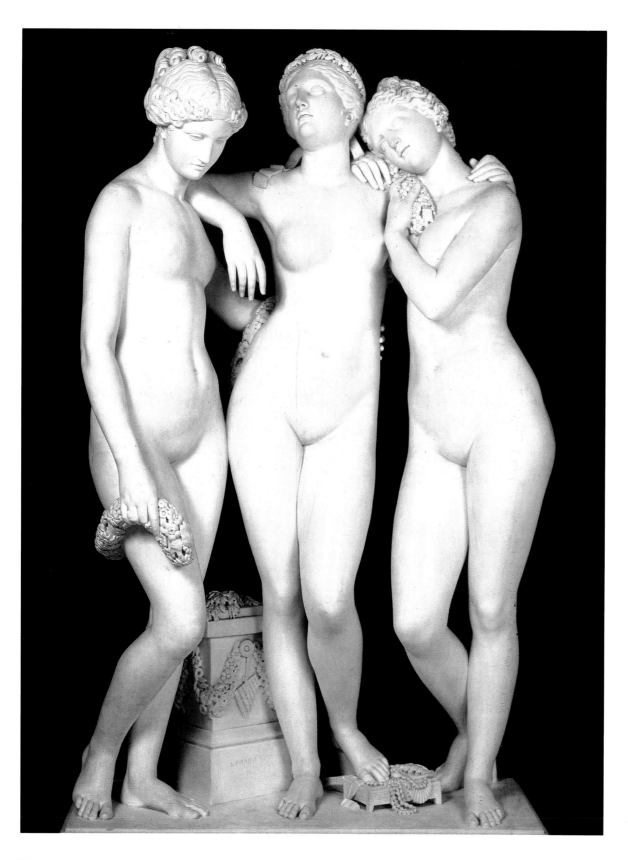

The Three Graces, *carved in marble by Jean Pradier, in another interpretation of an enduringly popular subject amongst Neoclassical sculptors. The classical theme is depicted with some sensuousness, as is often the case with sculpture of this time.*

THE LESSONS OF FRENCH REVOLUTIONARY ART

It might be difficult today to grasp the effect paintings and sculpture had on late eighteenth and early nineteenth century life, but they were regarded as capable of conveying strong moral or inspirational messages. Allegories, messages and inspiration were looked for in many of the paintings and sculptures executed at the time. The works of David, of course, were carefully studied, but attention also was given to artists like Louis Gauffier (1762–1801), whose historical painting, *Generosity of the Women of Rome* (1790), in which Roman women give their jewels to make a cup for Apollo, had been inspired by the gesture of French women artists who, in 1789, had left their jewels at the Assemblée Nationale to help the cause.

Likewise admired was Pierre-Narcisse Guérin (1744–1833), whose painting, *The Return of Marcus Sextus*, was exhibited in 1799 and hailed as conveying a counter-revolutionary message.

Later artists, such as François Gérard (1770–1837), who trained for a time in David's studio, seemed to lose much of the early revolutionaries' fevour. Gérard not only became portraitist to pillars of the Consulate and Empire, but also, under the Restoration, was named official painter of the newly restored monarchy, or Peintre des Rois.

Possibly the last of the Neoclassical artists was Jean-Auguste Dominique Ingres (1780–1867), whose œuvre, from the time he entered David's studio in 1797, spanned over six decades, moving from pure Neoclassicism to works that took French art well into the nineteenth century.

Jupiter and Thetis, *painted in Rome in 1806 by Jean-August Ingres. At 17 Ingres studied under David in Paris, but spent much of his later working life in Rome. Although both classical and Neoclassical references are present, this painting is far more sensuous than most others of the period.*

The Death of Caesar, *by Vincenzo Camuccini, who lived and worked in Rome. Historical paintings were a very popular genre.*

PAINTING IN ENGLAND IN THE NEOCLASSICAL ERA

During this time, there was not the same revolutionary fervour in England that there was in France, and domestic painting and sculpture reflected this difference. English painting in the late 1700s was considered naïve compared to that of France or Italy. The simplicity of the domesticated English squire, as painted by Arthur Devis or Johann Zoffany, was as far from the meaningful canvases of the Revolutionary painters as Worcestershire was from Versailles.

But although English air was not scented with revolution, there was a deep interest and understanding of the Antique in particular, and Neoclassicism in general. Sir Joshua Reynolds, the first president of the Royal Academy of Arts, England's answer to the Académie Française, was also an early member of the Society of Dilettanti. He went to Rome for two years, from 1750 until 1752, and like so many before him became imbued with the beauties of classical art. On his return to England, he became one of the few contemporary English painters who was also a critic and theorist. When the Royal Academy opened in 1769, Reynolds gave a series of fifteen Discourses on the Arts, which were widely read and highly influential.

Although history paintings were popular in England, the genre was less subscribed to there than on the Continent, mainly, thought Reynolds, because English Protestant churches were against excessive ornament and paintings, unlike their Catholic counterparts. However, artists like the American-born Benjamin West (1738–1820) and Swiss native Angelica Kauffmann (1741–1807), early members of the Royal Academy, were both famous for stirring works of classical endeavour that were admired by a wide public.

Left: The Coronation of the Emperor Napoleon and His Empress. *The Place de la Concorde is depicted as a Roman Forum – despite the modern touch in the balloons!*

Angelica Kauffmann, an engraving of a self-portrait. A painter of portraits, who lived much of her life in Rome, she was a founder member of the Royal Academy in England. Married to the artist Antonio Zucchi, she worked with him on commissions for several of Robert Adam's interiors.

Cup, cover and saucer, made by the Meissen factory near Dresden, the cup with a portrait of Angelica Kauffmann, and on the saucer a picture of Ariadne and Cupid after a painting by Kauffmann.

One painter working at the time in England represented a different facet of the Neoclassical era. Joseph Wright of Derby (1734–97) was a man whose interests represented the new Age of Enlightenment. A complex figure, albeit with a successful portrait business, he was a member of the interesting esoteric group, the Lunar Society, and many of his paintings reflected the concerns of that coterie of scientists and inventors. *A Philosopher Giving That Lecture on the Orrery, in which a Lamp is Put in Place of the Sun*, which Derby painted in 1766, and *An Experiment on a Bird in the Air Pump* (1768) both serve to sum up the spirit of that age, ever progressing in terms of art, science and industry.

Thomas Lawrence (1769–1830) epitomized the later Regency period in English Neoclassical art, with its Greek Revival background. He was elected to the Royal Academy in 1794 and became its president in 1820. His paintings reflected his interest in Greek Art and antiquities, and he became the secretary to the Society of Dilettanti in 1822, working on the later volumes of the Society's *Antiquities of Ionia*.

Sculpture in England was overshadowed by works produced in France and Italy, but one who found fame both at home and abroad was John Flaxman (1755–1826). He attended the academy schools in London, and by the time he was twenty was modelling cameos, friezes and portraits for Josiah Wedgwood's already popular Jasper ware. In 1787 Flaxman went to Rome, where he stayed for seven years. As an espouser of the supremacy of Greek art, he drew sets of illustrations for many of the great Greek works, which were much admired in their engraved form and used as inspiration by many of the great painters of the day.

The Orrery, *by Joseph Wright of Derby, one of several of his works that illustrated the spirit of scientific enquiry that prefaced the Industrial Revolution.*

Above: *Nelson's tomb in the crypt of St Paul's Cathedral, designed by John Flaxman. Flaxman made his reputation from his series of line engravings made in Rome, done as illustrations to classical literature, which were much used by painters and sculptors of the day.*

The Monument to the Convention Nationale in the Panthéon in Paris. Despite its individual figures being caught in movement, the work as a whole is carefully, even rigidly, composed and balanced.

III

NEOCLASSICAL PUBLIC ARCHITECTURE

THE FINEST ARCHITECTURAL ACHIEVEMENTS of the Greeks and Romans were their temples and public buildings. Created to worship both gods and men, they became ideal monuments to taste.

There were many differences between the architectural aspirations of the Ancient Greeks and the Romans. The simplicity of Greek architecture, wherein the public buildings were either temples or necessary places of meeting or learning, gave way to the more complex structures of Roman building. The massive vault of the Pantheon in Rome and the many arches of the aqueducts and bridges that straddled the country were typical of later Roman buildings. Triumphal arches, obelisks and pyramids—all structures that could be recognized at a distance—became beacons of the Empire's power and greatness.

By the time of the decline of Imperial Rome, buildings were being designed that not only showed the nation's power, but also that of an

The Massachusetts State House in Boston. Replacing an earlier simpler building designed in the 1720s, it was designed between 1795-8 by Charles Bulfinch, a native of Boston. The Neoclassical style has been much used for public buildings for the last two centuries.

individual, his wealth and standing in the community. Many ruined buildings throughout the original Roman Empire, from Ephesus to Verulamium (present-day St Albans) are still inscribed with the name of some worthy benefactor, eager to tell posterity of his wealth and importance.

After the fall of the Roman Empire, and the swamping of civilized Europe by many different barbarian tribes, the art of architecture went into decline for several centuries. It started to revive in about the tenth century, and developed from there—particularly in religious architecture—through both the Romanesque and Gothic styles to the great flowering of arts that came to be known as the Renaissance.

URBAN PUBLIC BUILDINGS
FROM THE RENAISSANCE ONWARDS

Fifteenth-century architects used their buildings—much as their forebears had done—to proclaim the greatness, grandeur and glory of their states, and to show their recently acquired knowledge of both the fine and applied arts, new and old. This dawning realization of the importance of public buildings also led the Italians to reassess the design of their cities. In *De Architectura*, the only extant treatise on Antique architecture, written by the Roman architect Vitruvius Pollio at the end of the first century BC, cities were shown as being designed to a plan, very often with all roads radiating from a central point, and with the major buildings sited and built in proportion to each other.

By the Middle Ages, however, the concept of the city in Europe had deteriorated to what was, in many cases, just a jumble of buildings, some large, some small. This urban hotchpotch had risen, as it were, amorphically, from dirty, squalid streets, as the city increased in size and importance.

By the seventeenth century, as knowledge was more widely shared, this big-village concept was changing everywhere. In the chaotic, smelly streets of London, where the change had been accelerated by the catastrophic Great Fire of 1666, old wooden buildings were replaced by stone edifices, built by great architects like John Vanbrugh and Christopher Wren.

THE NEW, NEOCLASSICAL CITY

This gradual process meant that by the eighteenth century the time was right for a new common vision of the city. Now it was felt that the urban centre should be viewed as a proud monument to the nation, with public buildings that spoke of virtues like purpose and civic responsibility, that eschewed excess and preferred simplicity. This new wish, both political and philosophical, coincided with a desire on the part of the artists to re-create the imposing architecture of the Ancients. The increasing interest in archaeology and excavation both in Italy and Greece had fired the imagination of many, and for the first time not only was the theory behind classical architecture being studied, but the original buildings were closely examined in order that classical principles could be applied to contemporary architecture.

There were stylistic reasons as well for the change, particularly on the Continent, where both the baroque and rococo styles had been used more widely, and in more extreme forms, than in England. The seductive charms of the rococo—its light decoration, delicate relief work and pale, clear colours—had in part replaced the heaviness of the baroque. But, like good comedy, the evanescent spirit of the rococo was difficult to sustain, and what began as a style both refreshing and pretty became, in time, cloying and overblown. The time was right for something new.

Neoclassicism affected different countries in different ways. There was, for example, no particular conscious return to the art of the classical in Italy. The Italians had, after all, never rejected it. From the earliest days of the Renaissance, Florence, Venice, Rome and the other great city-states had always employed Antique-inspired devices. With inspiration lying all around them, early Italian architects automatically incorporated classical ideas and ideals into their work, and continued to do so through the centuries. Although the mid-eighteenth century did see some fine examples of Neoclassical architecture, such as the works of Guiseppe Japelli (1783–1852), it was as a progression rather than a reaction.

PUBLIC BUILDINGS IN FRANCE

In France, too, from the time of the Renaissance there had been a tradition of grand public building. Louix XIV started a programme of building that not only affected public places, but also ensured the gradual expansion of Paris; indeed, a century later, the city had spread so much as to comprise virtually two towns, the new and the old. Geographically well placed to benefit from Italy's craftsmen and painters, French architects throughout the seventeenth century experimented with classical structures and ornament. This was not because of any particular interest in the principles or philosophy of the Greeks and Romans, but more a desire to incorporate the various Antique devices into the fabric of their new buildings.

By the 1600s, France was the most powerful and the richest country in Europe, and its buildings reflected this. Ruled by monarchs with an abiding interest in architecture as an expression of their own power, many things were done to perpetuate the grand growth of France. In 1635 Cardinal Richelieu founded the Académie de France to promote and countinue the nation's artistic traditions. In 1671 Jean-Baptiste Colbert, Louis XIV's Chief Minister and a man driven with the perception of France's grandeur, founded the Académie Royale d'Architecture, under the control of the Surintendant des Bâtiments du Roi. Every year the students of the Académie presented drawings for the Prix de Rome competition, and those who won the prestigious Grand Prix were sent to the Académie de France à Rome for three years, to study painting and archaeology.

The Interior of the Pantheon in Rome during the eighteenth century, a painting from the studio of Giovanni Paolo Pannini. Built around the first century as a temple it was used as such until consecrated as a church in 608 by Pope Boniface IV. The top of the dome is a single circular opening which floods the whole building with light. Panini was the first artist to paint antiquities, and his work was quickly in huge demand.

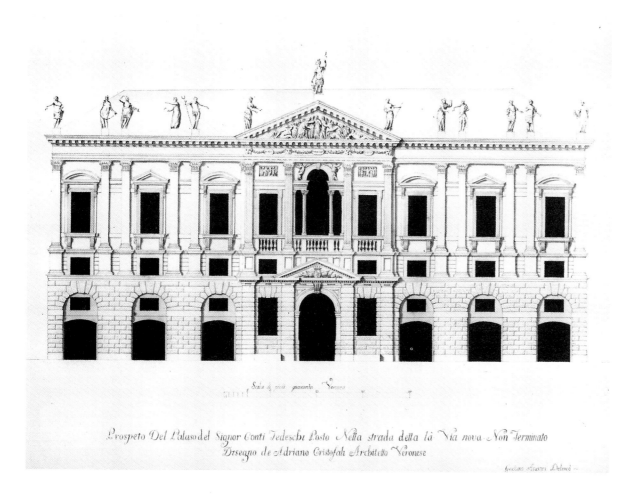

Prospeto Del Palaso del Signor Conti Tedeschi Posto Nella strada della là Via nova Non Terminato
Diseqno de Adriano Cristofali Architetto Veronese

The façade of the Conti Palace. In Italy early Neoclassicism was less a new movement, more a continuation of the old.

Louis XIV, the Sun King, who reigned from 1643 to 1715 and whose glory was purposely reflected through the architecture of France, increased both the pace of building and the monumentalism of their designs. Although the baroque reigned supreme, Colbert had sent Antoine Desgodetz to Rome to measure 49 of the city's ruined monuments; *Antiques edifices de Rome*, the result of his work, was published in 1682.

GABRIEL, FRANCE'S FIRST NEOCLASSICAL ARCHITECT

Ange-Jacques Gabriel (1698–1782), who was born during the reign of Louis XIV and became known as the first important Neoclassical architect in France, was a direct link in the chain from baroque to rococo to Neoclassicism. He, singularly, never went to Rome, but instead came to architecture via an establishment route, following the path of his father, who had been Premier Architecte du Roi to Louis XV, and himself becoming the Chief Architect to the same king in 1742. He worked only for Louis, and designed in several different styles. His lack of Roman experience did not mean he was not a follower of the classic ideal. During his tenure as Premier Architecte du Roi, and until his death, Gabriel designed some of the major public buildings in Paris, like the Ecole Militaire, and in 1755 was responsible for the monumental grandeur of the Place Louis XV, better known now as the Place de la Concorde.

SOUFFLOT AND THE MARQUIS DE MARIGNY

Although there were several other early prophets of the Neoclassical style in France—like the Italian, Giovanni Niccolò Servandoni, whose design for the façade of St Sulpice in 1732 was a forerunner of the Neoclassical style—possibly the first architect after Gabriel to design an instantly recognizable Neoclassical building was Jacques-Germain Soufflot (1713–80). He was the architect of the church of Paris's patron saint, Ste Geneviève, known as the Panthéon since the Revolution.

The young Soufflot spent seven years in Rome, at the Académie de France, arriving there when he was eighteen. When he returned to France, he became municipal architect of Lyons, building the Loge-au-Change and the façade of the Hôtel-Dieu. This last work apparently brought Soufflot to the attention of Mme de Pompadour (1721–64). Although usually associated with the rococo, Louix XV's mistress actually encouraged, and even accelerated, the pace of Neoclassicism in France because of her

The interior of the Panthéon in Paris, designed by J.-G. Soufflot between 1756 and 1790. Giant Corinthian columns divided the nave from the aisles, but the building shows various stylistic influences: Byzantine, Gothic and Baroque, as well as Roman.

interest in architecture and her advancement of both her brother and her uncle, Charles-François Lenormant de Tournehem, to the influential post of Directeur Général des Bâtiments du Roi.

In 1749 Mme de Pompadour asked Soufflot to accompany her brother, Abel-François Poisson (1727–81), then the Marquis de Vandières—whom she hoped to promote to the prestigious post of Directeur des Bâtiments—on his Grand Tour, in company with Charles-Nicolas Cochin, the engraver and critic, and the Abbé Le Blanc. They visited the usual, by now mandatory, sights suitable for young noble gentlemen, but also, somewhat unusually, visited the ancient Greek site of Paestum, near Naples, where Soufflot measured the dimensions of the Doric temples. Much later, in 1764, he produced a publication on them, which had a marked influence on the study of Greek architecture as opposed to everything Roman, adding fuel to the fiery debate about which was the finer.

Later, back in France, the Marquis de Vandières, now with the title Marquis de Marigny, who had been made Directeur des Bâtiments in 1751, asked Soufflot to design Ste-Geneviève. Soufflot carried out the commission with a domed circular building in the monumental classical style which was at that time considered revolutionary.

PARIS'S SCHOOLS OF ARCHITECTURE

Paris was fortunate in its architectural schools. As well as the Académie Royale d'Architecture, from 1743 the city had an independent school of architecture, L'Ecole des Arts, founded by Jean-François Blondel (1705–74). Soon to become one of the most influential schools of architecture in the eighteenth century, the school thrived for nearly twenty years until Blondel became Professeur at the Académie Royale. As well as running the school, Blondel published *Cours d'architecture*, a seven-part work that appeared over a six-year period (the last sections were published posthumously in 1777). These widely read volumes ensured that his teaching would influence not only the first, but several succeeding generations of new architects.

Many of France's finest Neoclassical architects studied with Blondel, and he was responsible for training most of the first wave—men like Charles Michel-Ange Challe, Jean-Laurent Le Geay and Louis-Joseph Le Lorrain among them—as well as the possibly more prolific second wave of Neoclassical architects. These were men like Claude-Nicholas Ledoux, Jean-François de Neufforge, Marie-Joseph Peyre, Charles de Wailly and the English architect William Chambers, whose doctrines soon dominated

The Rotonde at the Parc Monceau, built for the Anglophile Duc de Chartres. The Rotonde was designed by C.-N. Ledoux.

early Neoclassical teaching in England. Also there during that period was Charles-Louis Clérisseau, a painter who was to exert considerable influence over Robert Adam and others. Most of these young architects had also spent some time in Rome in the years between 1740 and 1760. In Italy, they all became part of large, homogeneous group—some Academicians, some not, but all active artists and architects, working to find out as much as possible about the Antique world around them.

CLÉRISSEAU, THE COMMUNICATOR

The story of Charles-Louis Clérisseau (1721–1820) is instructive if only because he represents the incredible communication of ideas and personalities that went on at such a remarkable time, in so rich an environment. Clérisseau was an artist who spent most of his working life in Rome between 1749 and 1756. When he was twenty-eight, he was sent to study and live as a *pensionnaire* as the Académie de France à Rome for five years. Then, although he left the academy, he stayed on in Rome for several more years. When William Chambers was in Italy, from 1750, it was Clérisseau who instructed him. After Chambers had returned to England, Clérisseau met Robert Adam in 1755, then six months into his Grand Tour and anxious to absorb as much of Rome as he could. For a couple of years, according to John Fleming in *Robert Adam and His Circle*, Clérisseau and Adam spent much time together, the former teaching his charge to draw, giving him introductions and arranging expeditions to places like Herculaneum and Spalatro. On the strength of the latter visit, Adam published a highly successful book, *The Ruins of Spalatro*, in 1764. Five years later, Clérisseau similarly took James Adam, Robert's brother, under his wing.

Clérisseau's skill, or gift, was one of communication. Everyone of note seemed to have met him, and he seemed to know everyone there was to know. And his influence spread farther than Europe. Clérisseau visited a Roman temple, the Maison Carrée, at Nîmes with Thomas Jefferson, then travelling in Europe, and drew plans of it for him. Jefferson then based the new Virginia State Capital at Richmond on Clérisseau's design. Charles Cameron, too, who designed much of the Neoclassical palace of Tsarskoe Selo for Catherine the Great, was apparently employed after a recommendation to the Empress from Clérisseau.

THE CONSTANT LURE OF ROME

Rome at this time was not a large city, and it housed a constantly shifting foreign community. Clérisseau seemed to live there long enough to see, and get to know, most of the travellers. As late as 1787 he was still being talked about in Rome, as even Goethe, in his letters from Italy, mentions him.

Between 1750 and 1760, many of the now Neoclassically disposed architects returned to France from Rome, and their influence was soon felt. The Seven Years' War with England—a period during which neither the French nor English were exposed to the architectural influences of the other—ended in 1763, and there was immediately a rush of new building, both public and private, on both sides of the English Channel.

The Maison Carrée at Nîmes, constructed by the Romans in 16 BC. Wonderfully preserved, it has been the inspiration for many architects including, famously, Thomas Jefferson, who was so struck by its beauty that he used the plans as a basis for his Virginia Capitol.

Marie-Joseph Peyre (1730–85), for example, a student of the Académie, went to Rome after winning the Grand Prix with a design for a public fountain. Peyre returned to Paris from Rome in 1756 and built, six years later, the Hôtel Leprêtre de Neubourg at Clos Payen, south of Paris, in a strict Neoclassical style. In 1765 he published *Oeuvres d'architecture*, which not only showed buildings like the Baths of Diocletian and the Pantheon, but also included designs for contemporary Neoclassical interiors. He later designed, with de Wailly, the Théâtre de l'Odéon (1779–85).

Charles de Wailly (1730–98) in Paris won the Grand Prix in 1752. In Rome he became involved in archaeological excavations with Pierre-Louis Moreau-Desproux (later the Surintendant des Bâtiments in Paris, 1763–87) and others. On his return to Paris, he opened an atelier where he taught a number of fledgling architects, including the Russians Ivan Starov, Fiodor Volkhov and Vasili Bazhenov, who later returned to Russia.

There was also Jean-François Chalgrin (1739–1811), who travelled to Rome when he was twenty. On his return to France, he became Inspecteur des Travaux de la Ville de Paris, under Moreau-Desproux. His design of the Arc de Triomphe (1806–35) was as much influenced by Roman triumphal arches as anything yet seen. In its massiveness and its dominating position, it celebrated military victory in a way any Roman emperor would have envied.

A link between the traditional classicism of earlier architects and the almost revolutionary ideas of men like Ledoux was Jacques Gondoin (1757–1818), the son of Louis XV's gardener. His design for the Ecole de Chirurgie, between 1769 and 1774, combined the classicism of Roman monuments like the Pantheon with an understanding of the rational, ordered approach that underlay the expanding scientific disciplines—in this instance, surgery.

BOULLÉE AND LEDOUX

It might have been that this exposure to real classicism blunted somewhat the searching, creative side of the Neoclassical movement, for possibly the most revolutionary of all French Neoclassicists were two men who never went to Italy at all, Boullée and Ledoux. Etienne-Louis Boullée (1728–99), the elder of the two, wielded his influence almost entirely through his designs and his teaching, the latter taking place at his atelier, where his students included Alexandre-Théodore Brogniart, Chalgrin and Peyre. His Neoclassicism became almost abstract, culminating in his (unrealized) 1784 monument to Sir Isaac Newton, an enormous empty sphere enclosing a planetarium and Newton's shrine.

Claude-Nicholas Ledoux (1736–1806), on the other hand, passed his early career as a much sought after, fashionable Neoclassicist, designing several grand, even somewhat ostentatious, Parisian houses. In 1772, he

Right: *The Rotonde de la Villette. One of the forty barrières, or toll-houses, built by Claude Ledoux from 1785 to 1789, it was based on the classical, but, as with much of Ledoux's later work, taken beyond. Designed to stand on the major routes into Paris, the toll-houses, of which only four remain, encircled the capital.*

Etienne-Louis Boullée's unbuilt monument to Isaac Newton.

designed the Pavillon de Louveciennes for the Comtesse du Barry, the dressmaker's daughter who became Louix XV's mistress. Created with a great understanding of the Neoclassical idiom, the Pavillon put the seal on Ledoux's success, and he was named Architecte du Roi in 1773. More revolutionary designs began to evolve in the 1770s. His famous saltworks, the Saline de Chaux at Arc-et-Senans, built between 1775 and 1779, is a massive, forceful design, incorporating baseless banded columns, cubes, cylinders and spheres. One of his last, and certainly one of his most controversial, works was the design and building of a series of the *barrières*, or customs posts, guarding all entries to Paris. Each pavilion was different in design, but from all emanated a sense of strength and power, emphasized by heavy columns and classical designs.

The example of Boullée, and the fact that his influence was mainly transmitted through unrealized designs, illustrates another feature of eighteenth-century architecture, Neoclassical and otherwise. Not only were there thousands of words written during the 1700s and early 1800s on the subject, there were also thousands of drawings and designs produced for buildings that were never commissioned, and never would be. Due in part to the intermittent wars and even revolutions that curtailed building activities, these designs had a disproportionate effect on the reputations of their creators, and many architects were considered distinguished on the strength of folios of never-realized designs. The Grand Prix of the Académie de France—the winners of which were sent to Rome as *pensionnaires*—was won for designs, and indeed some architects were known almost solely for these drawings. The never-built mausoleum by William Chambers for Frederick, Prince of Wales, who died in 1751, and the unrealized monument for Frederick the Great designed by David Gilly in Berlin made both these architects famous among their peers. Claude-Nicholas Ledoux's later reputation as a revolutionary architect was based almost solely on buildings that were never built, in particular those for Chaux, the ideal New Town, which he conceived in 1775. He also published a book after the Revolution (having actually been imprisoned for a time), using pure unadorned geometric shapes in a manner that seems modern today.

THE EMPIRE STYLE,
AND PERCIER AND FONTAINE

The French Revolution naturally brought a temporary halt to the construction of Neoclassical or indeed any other type of architecture in France, but the rise of Napoleon meant a new confidence and impetus in building. Napoleon called himself Emperor, and was quick to invent a parallel between his reign and those of the mighty emperors of the past. Once again, public architecture would herald the might of the leader, and a new confident strain of Neoclassicism, the Empire style, was born. Buildings like the Bourse, designed by Brongniart, and the Madeleine, a new temple, were outward manifestations of the emperor's greatness, and, in case anyone should mistake the analogy, Jacques Gondoin's Colonne de la Grande Armée in the Place Vendôme was closely modelled Trajan's column in Rome, built to record his many victories.

Charles Percier (1764–1838) and Pierre-François-Léonard Fontaine (1762–1853) are known to most as the progenitors of the Empire style,

renowned as much for their widely reproduced book, *Recueil des décorations intérieures*, published in 1801, as for their actual architectural work. The book included designs for specific furniture and schemes for rooms, nearly all based on the pair's rather romantic view of Ancient Rome. Percier and Fontaine had both studied in Rome in the 1780s, and upon their return to Paris in 1791, they joined forces and became designers at the Opéra, although the Revolution brought that to an end. After the success of their book, they worked on decorative schemes for the new leaders of Revolutionary France, until in 1802 they came to Napoleon's attention, and after that, until 1814, worked only for him. The commissions were both personal and public, incorporating both decorative and architectural schemes. They built the Arc de Triomphe du Carousel, based on the arch of Septimius Severus, as a gateway between the Louvre and the Tuileries, and also worked on the royal châteaux, in particular Malmaison. Their public and urban works, like the Rue de Rivoli, all projected the same grandeur and might of the State, and by inference, Napoleon.

Left: *The Palais Bourbon, which, over many years, was the subject of both schemes and additions by several architects including Boullée, and later, Bernard Poyet, who added the classical portico in 1808.*

The Bourse in Paris, designed by A.-T. Brongniart. He started it in 1807, and it was altered and enlarged in 1895. Brogniart was also the architect of the monumental cemetery Père-Lachaise.

La Madeleine church in Paris was originally to be built, in 1761, by the classical architect Contant d'Ivry. But only the foundations were raised, and the church was not finished until the next century, when Alexandre-Pierre Vignon built an imposing Roman temple raised on a podium, between 1807 and 1845.

The Petit Trianon at Versailles built by Ange-Jacques Gabriel for Madame de Pompadour, but which she never lived to see completed. Elegant and dignified, it marked the transition from the Rococo to Neoclassicism.

INFLUENTIAL WRITINGS ON NEOCLASSICISM

Both French and Germans academics, ever ready to theorize, thought and wrote profusely on the intellectual side of Neoclassicism, much of which influenced subsequent architects. From Blondel and his *Cours d'architecture* on, many architects, designers and professors wrote innumerable essays, treatises and *pensées* between 1700 and 1820. Chief, and most influential among them all, were the works of Marc-Antoine Laugier (1713–69), who was not even an architect but a Jesuit priest. His great work, *Essai sur l'architecture*, was published in 1753; in it, he condemned ornament and decoration for their own sake, and viewed classical architecture as the original and only truth, pre-eminent in its simplicity.

Various aspects of Neoclassicism were explored in these prolific writings. Jean-François de Neufforge (1714–91) began publishing the eight-volume *Recueil élémentaire d'architecture* in 1757, and it appeared over an eleven-year period. The designs ranged from theatres to villas, and the books became the Neoclassical manual for two generations of architects; the Petit Trianon, designed by Gabriel, is said to be based on engravings from the work. The year 1780 saw the publication of *Le Génie de l'architecture; ou l'analogie de cet art avec nos sensations*, written by Nicholas Le Camus de Mezières and expounding the aesthetic pleasures of architecture. The German scholar Winckelmann, based in Rome from 1755, wrote several important treatises proclaiming his views on the superiority of Hellenic art to Roman. Many of these books were still in circulation some hundred years later, instructing and edifying subsequent generations of architects. In England, too there were significant

publications: in 1756, Isaac Ware, a Palladian and follower of Lord Burlington, published his *Complete Body of Architecture*, which made a plea for a return to basics, and William Chambers' *Treatise on Civil Architecture* (1759) was read closely in Britain for many years.

NEOCLASSICAL PUBLIC BUILDINGS IN BRITAIN

As always, the British Isles were more isolated from mainstream movements, both architectural and political. The baroque style, for example, did not have the impact in England that it did on the Continent. It was not that England eschewed the baroque. It just adopted a different form. During the seventeenth century, the particular baroque works of Wren, Vanbrugh and Inigo Jones—very different from those of their French contemporaries—had ruled supreme. Not until the early 1700s did Neoclassicism begin to touch churches and other edifices.

As far as state buildings were concerned, the English looked more to the simplicity of design that they felt they achieved with their country estates. The idea of a simple, dignified house, built along classical lines and standing in a natural setting, was carried into the public domain. There was one similarity with France, however, in that its capital was growing faster than before. Horace Walpole remembered that on a visit to London in the 1740s, his father could not place himself because of the number of new streets and squares that had been built since his last visit. By 1776, it looked, he thought, as if 'they had imported two or three capitals. London could put Florence into its fob-pocket . . . rows of houses shoot out every way like a polypus.'

And so at the beginning of the Neoclassical movement, the Palladian ideal, which in itself was based on classical models, persisted for public buildings as much as it had for private.

The classical held sway for the remainder of the eighteenth century, whether in the guise of early Palladianism or later, as a more romantically inspired genre. As late as 1809 John Soane was exhorting students at the Royal Academy that

> . . . the student be fully acquainted with the different forms and constructions of ancient Temples. In them he will discover many of the great principles of his art; in them he will learn many of the laws of composition. He will observe the beauty of form, and the correct application of the sublime to architecture, the effect of the whole being so well understood in these great works.

One of the earliest architects to incorporate classical structures into his work, a man who was much admired at the time, was James Gibbs (1682–1754). Primarily a church architect, the Aberdeen-born Gibbs built the circular Radcliffe Library at Oxford and in London the little St Peter's in Vere Street (originally a chapel-of-ease for Lord Oxford), St Mary-le-Strand and the new St Martin-in-the-Fields, which replaced an earlier church. This last was finished in 1726, and its Corinthian columns and pediment, as well as its fine interior, made it very expensive for the time, costing over £60,000, of which £33,000 was granted by Parliament and the rest raised by voluntary contributions.

St Martin-in-the-Fields, London, built by architect James Gibbs in 1722-6. Although contemporary with the Palladians, he followed a different avenue of classical architecture.

PALLADIANISM, PATRONAGE AND BURLINGTON

There was at that time no equivalent of the Académie Royale de l'Architecture in England, nor a private school of the calibre of that of Blondel, although six years after the 1768 founding of the Royal Academy, a travelling scholarship was offered to gold medal winners by the Society of Dilettanti. Most of the young architects, painters and scholars who arrived in Rome and Athens were sent by their patrons—rich collectors and scholars, with interests in both the Antique and archaeology—and many of them were later members of the Society of Dilettanti.

Chief among these patrons was a man who, although untaught, was as much an architect as any of the professionals with whom he worked. Richard Boyle, the 3rd Earl of Burlington, is generally recognized as one of the first discoverers and disciples of Palladianism. His passion for Andrea Palladio's writings and designs, which he saw when travelling in Italy in 1719, affected a generation of both architects and buildings. London had already seen the first publication of Palladio's *Works*, published in 1715 by an Italian, Giacomo Leoni, and translated by Nicholas Dubois. After Burlington's second trip to Italy, he brought back a copy of *Fabbriche Antiche Disegnate da Andrea Palladio*, which he published in 1730. *Vitruvius Britannicus*, by the Scottish architect, Colen Campbell (1673–1729), was also published at about the same time, and this volume greatly impressed Burlington, prompting him to ask Campbell to work on his own town house, Burlington House in Piccadilly.

Burlington was not, however, just another rich nobleman playing at design. Horace Walpole, not always the most charitable of men when discussing his contemporaries, thought Burlington a good architect and mentioned his work in York and a dormitory at Westminster School that the peer had designed. He considered his buildings 'more chaste and classic than [William] Kent's'—obviously not a comment about an amateur. The York project was the new Assembly Rooms, begun in 1730 and finished in 1736. The rooms supposedly derived from a mixture of elements, including Palladio's reconstruction of a hall 'in the manner of the Egyptians' that Palladio himself had based on a description in Vitruvius, combined with another, separate, passage on the courtyard of a Greek house.

Palladian fever, although embraced more heartily for private houses, also took hold in the public domain. Other early Palladians included John Wood (1704–54) of Bath and his son—also John Wood (1728–81)—who between them constructed most of the then revolutionary sweeping terraces and crescents of Georgian Bath. Town planning on this scale, with each element designed as part of a majestic whole, had not been seen before in England, and although John Wood the Elder died before completing his original scheme, his son continued his work and built the Royal Crescent, still one of the most magnificent examples of urban design extant, although father and son's complete plans were never to be realized in full.

The Completion of the Royal Crescent in Bath in 1769, *painted in watercolour by Thomas Malton the Younger. The Woods, father and son, were the first true town planners; although their classically inspired terraces in Bath are universally admired, they were, in fact, but part of a much larger scheme which was never completed.*

A SECOND WAVE OF NEOCLASSICISM

Startling as it was at the time, the Palladian movement as exemplified by Lord Burlington in the early 1700s gave way, around mid-century, to a second wave of Neoclassicism. This *nouvelle vague* owed far less to the theories of Palladio and far more to first-hand knowledge of the Ancient world. There was now a new generation of English architects, men who had travelled widely and knew the buildings of the Ancient world from direct experience, not just from books and engravings.

Towards the middle of the eighteenth century, two important British architects, both of whom were to work in a classical mode, came back to England at about the same time from their sojourns in Rome. These were William Chambers, who returned in 1755, and Robert Adam, who arrived back three years later.

CHAMBERS, THE PAN-EUROPEAN ARCHITECT

William Chambers (1723–96) can really be considered one of the first pan-European architects, for as well as studying in Rome for several years, he was also enrolled, prior to that, in 1749–50, at Blondel's famous Ecole des Arts in Paris. It was an important period at the school, a time when major architects of the future like de Wailly and Peyre were studying there. From Paris Chambers went to Rome in 1750, where he stayed and then married in 1753. For five years he and his wife lived and worked in Rome, knowing intimately, and being influenced by both Piranesi and Clérisseau.

Chambers was also unusual for this time, in that, although a European—probably more so than any of his contemporaries—he was also an establishment man, preferring the patronage of the royal family to that sense of almost semi-republicanism that many of his contemporaries felt. Patronized by, and architectural tutor to, the Prince of Wales, later King George III, he designed a wide range of royal and non-royal commissions, including the Pagoda in Kew Gardens, the State Coach and of course several houses. He was knighted by George III in 1770, and named, first, Architect of Works (1761) and then Surveyor General to the Office of Works (1782). His career culminated in his greatest public work, Somerset House, London, which was begun in 1777 and completed in 1801, after Chambers' death.

Opposite: *The Great Hall at Syon House on the western outskirts of London. The sixteenth-century house was extensively remodelled in the Palladian style by Robert Adam in 1761. The elegant purity of Adam's Neoclassicism had a revolutionary impact on architecture elsewhere—notably in France, Russia and America.*

The Great Subscription Room at Brooks' Club, St James's in London, in an engraving. It was designed by Henry Holland in 1776-8. His architectural style, whilst still Neoclassical, was more European in flavour than that of many of his contemporaries. He went on to design Carlton House, now demolished, for the Prince of Wales.

In 1751 Chambers wrote a classic work, *A Treatise on Civil Architecture*, outlining the five orders and their use in architecture, which was reprinted three times in his lifetime alone. Although never original, in terms of experimentation and imagination, Chambers' work was academically and classically correct, and was highly thought of, as it still is. John Soane's words still ring true, that 'the fame of Sir William Chambers will live as long as the work remains...'

ROBERT ADAM, ARCHITECT-DECORATOR

A man like Chambers, who both belonged to the establishment and was an academic, was anathema to someone like Robert Adam (1728–92), who had been in Rome slightly later than Chambers, spent much time with Clérisseau and then returned to England in 1758 to build up a practice in London. It is no secret that William Chambers was not a fan of Robert Adam; he considered him overrated, and his style lightweight and without proper regard to the Antique. It is no secret either that Adam considered Chambers his greatest rival, and constantly watched to see what he might do next, which commissions he would be offered and by whom. Their rivalry lasted as long as they were both working, and the fact that they were made joint Architects to the Office of Works in 1761 did not exactly please either of them.

Adam's fame rests with the work he did in private houses, both architecturally and decoratively, although he did undertake some public commissions, such as the Admiralty Screen in Whitehall, which he designed in 1759. Much later, he returned to his native Scotland to design the General Register House and the University of Edinburgh, both of which were completed posthumously.

The link connecting these eighteenth-century Neoclassical architects continued with Henry Holland (1745–1806), who in 1771 became the assistant of Capability Brown (and his son-in-law two years later), who was then adding architectural commissions to his gardening designs. Influenced by the work of both Chambers and Adam, Holland, who later taught John Soane, designed the classical Brooks' Club in St. James's, of which the Prince of Wales was a member, and went on to design the new Carlton House for the Prince.

The Church of All Hallows, London Wall. Inspired by the Roman Baths, it was built by George Dance the Younger between 1765 and 1767, as his first commission, on returning from Rome in 1764.

THE FINAL STAGE OF NEOCLASSICISM IN BRITAIN

By this time there was a new and perhaps the final phase of genuine Neoclassicism emerging, propagated by a new generation of architects, essentially men influenced by Adam and Chambers but not beholden to them. These younger architects, born in the middle of the eighteenth century, had been to Rome and, on returning to England, pushed the concept of Neoclassicism farther than it had been extended before. No longer merely involved with reproducing the patterns of the Ancients, these men used spaces and shapes in a much bolder, more modern way, particularly in their public works.

One of this new generation of architects was George Dance the younger (1741–1825), who went to Rome when he was seventeen and stayed for five years. Some of the more revolutionary French architects were still there, as were Piranesi and Clérisseau. On his return Dance was commissioned to build the church of All Hallows at London Wall (1765–67), and he became a member of the Royal Academy in 1768, at the young age of 27. He succeeded his father as Clerk of City Works and built Newgate prison (1769–78), a huge structure that moved towards the more monumental lines of later European Neoclassicism.

James Wyatt (1747–1813) went to Italy in 1762, and he remained there for six years. Although perhaps best known for his Gothic work, in particular the light and fantastic lines of Horace Walpole's Strawberry Hill, he was also very successful as a Neoclassical architect, taking on Chambers' job as Surveyor General in 1796 on his death, and building prestigious commissions in the classical mode. His first famous undertaking was the Pantheon in Oxford Street. Elaborately designed balls and parties, with tickets by subscription, were very fashionable at this time, and the Pantheon, with its lofty domed interior, was designed for just such events. It was to prove a popular building with the public at large, despite this report from Caroline Lybbe Powys after the opening night that it was inferior to Ranelagh as a diversion: 'As there being so many rooms, no communication with the galleries, the staircase inconvenient, all rather contribute to lose the company than show them to advantage.'

Horace Walpole gave a jaundiced description of a rather bosky celebration at the Pantheon, held there seven years after its completion, in 1779:

> The company was first shut into the galleries to look down on the supper, then let to descend to it. Afterwards they were led into the subterraneous apartment, which was laid with mould and planted with trees, and crammed with nosegays: but the fresh earth, and the dead leaves, and the effluvia of breaths, made such a stench and moisture, that they were suffocated; and when they remounted, the legs and wings of chickens and remnants of ham (for the supper was not removed) poisoned them more. A druid in an arbour distributed verses to the ladies; the Baccelli and the dancers of the opera danced; and then danced the company; and then it being morning, and the candles burnt out, the windows were opened; and then the stewed danced assembly were such shocking figures, that they fled like ghosts, as they looked.

The reconstructed interior of the Bank Stock Office, Bank of England, originally completed by John Soane in 1793. The simple, even austere, decoration reflects Soane's emphasis on the most severe aspects of Neoclassicism.

Chambers' influence was to spread far wider than the confines of England. One of his pupils, James Gandon (1743–1823), became known as one of the architects of the glories of Georgian Dublin. His designs for the Custom House and the Four Courts, among other buildings, are some of the most admired in the city.

JOHN SOANE: AN ORIGINAL

John Soane (1753–1837), the last—and undoubtedly the most original—of these new Romans, occupied a class of his own. As revolutionary in his way as the French architects Ledoux and Boullée, Soane was influenced both by French thought and English architects.

Working first for Dance and later for Holland, Soane received King George III's Travelling Scholarship in 1778 and went to Italy for two years. Although he designed many private houses during his working life, after he returned to England he was appointed, in 1788, Surveyor to the Bank of England, for whom he worked over the next thirty years, ever adapting and redesigning. His designs, however, were not straightforward copies of Antiquity, nor of Palladio for that matter. A combination of geometry and poetry, illusions of space that are achieved by unusual structure, and an extraordinary use of light, make Soane as modern an architect as one could encounter today. He was showered with honour through his life, and among his laurels were a professorship at the Royal Academy in 1806 and a knighthood in 1831.

Downing College, Cambridge was designed by William Wilkins in Greek revival style, of which he was one of the leading nineteenth century exponents. He employed the style in other architectural designs for public buildings - in particular, the National Gallery in London.

THE GREEK REVIVAL IN BRITAIN

There had always been followers of the Greek in England. James 'Athenian' Stuart and Nicolas Revett, after their pioneering 1762 publication, *Antiquities of Athens*, had sparked the interest of many who had until then thought that all Antiquity emanated from Rome. The first known Greek building in England was James Stuart's representation of a temple in Lord Lyttelton's famous garden at Hagley. The second volume of *Antiquities of Athens*, edited by Stuart alone, appeared in 1789. Nearly twenty years later Lord Elgin brought his Parthenon marbles to London, and in 1807 William Wilkins (1778–1839), champion of the Greek Revival, published *Antiquities of Magna Graecia*, this after a three-year trip through Asia Minor, Greece and Italy.

The beginning of the nineteenth century witnessed a renewed interest in Greek architecture, promulgated by people like Thomas Hope, the collector, designer and critic. This 'Grecophilia' was given expression in one last, sometimes ponderous, phase of English Neoclassicism, the Greek Revival. Buildings like Wilkins' Downing College, Cambridge, which was started in 1806, Robert Smirke's massive British Museum (1823–47) and Wilkins' National Gallery (1834–38) all gave homage, if sometimes rather humourlessly, to Greece.

The Fitzwilliam Museum, Cambridge. The building was designed by George Basevi in 1834, but it was taken over on his death in 1845 by the archaeologist-architect, C. R. Cockerell. Cockerell was an expert on the Antique, and had worked on many excavations in Greece between 1810 and 1917.

Right: *The British Museum, London's purest Greek Revival public building, designed by Robert Smirke in 1824 and slowly built over the next twenty years. It was considered appropriate that the first national museum to display antiquities should be designed in classical style.*

One of the greatest town planners of the early nineteenth century was John Nash (1752–1835). Considered brilliant by some and a lightweight by others, he was not a pure Neoclassicist, for he designed in a multitude of styles. His Neoclassical genius was seen, though, in the sweep of streets and terraces that he designed for the centre of London, and although working in the early nineteenth century, as a Neoclassicist Nash was much more than a strict Greek Revivalist.

In 1810 he was asked to submit plans for development for the Marylebone district. His finished designs made a picturesque sweeping route between the Prince of Wales' residence, Carlton House, and the Regent's Park. Although much has been demolished of his original scheme, the classical villas and colonnaded terraces that remain give an idea of the breadth of scale in which he worked.

Cumberland Terrace in Regent's Park, London. Designed, with other classical terraces and villas, by John Nash in 1826, it was one of the highlights of an ambitious scheme to link Carlton House in the south with the Park in the north, linked by a suitably regal Regent Street. Now only All Souls church, Langham Place, remains of the plan.

Esplanade Row from the Chouringhee Road, Calcutta (after James Baillie Fraser, 1815). Colonial building across the wide British Empire followed the Neoclassical style that had proved so suitable for public life.

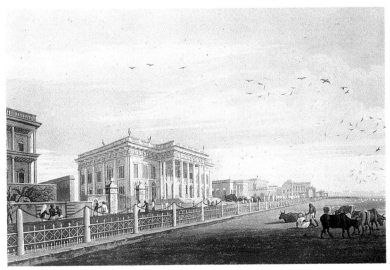

NEOCLASSICISM IN SCOTLAND

The classical tradition began far earlier in Scotland than Edinburgh's nineteenth-century sobriquet, 'Athens of the North', would imply. By the 1720s, when the work of William Adam (1689–1748)—architect and father of Robert and James—became fashionable, there was as much knowledge in Scotland Vitruvius and Palladio as there was further south.

William Adam started life as a mason but soon graduated to architecture, at which he was enormously successful. Although much of his work was done privately, he designed several public buildings, all in a relatively austere Palladian manner. In Glasgow, he designed the University Library (1732), a small Roman building complete with portico and alcoves for statues. In Edinburgh, he designed the Orphan Hospital (1734), and in 1738 both George Watson's Hospital and the Royal Infirmary.

Nearly one hundred years later, Edinburgh flourished again under a new impetus, that of the Greek Revival. Thomas Hamilton (1784–1858) was a Grecian enthusiast whose design for the Royal High School (1825–29) was a veritable but severe temple of learning. The later Royal College of Physicians (1844–46) was still grand, but built in a less monumental fashion. The name of William Henry Playfair (1789–1857) is strongly associated with this northern Athens. After winning a competition in 1817 to complete Robert Adam's Edinburgh University, which he did by 1824, Playfair designed a series of public buildings, including the New Observatory on Calton Hill (1818), the Royal Scottish Academy (1822) and the Surgeons' Hall (1829). Although each differed from the others, the combined œuvre gave an overriding sense of the Greek Revival to the city's New Town that was to be seen simultaneously in other countries of Europe.

The Royal High School in Edinburgh, now the Scottish Office building, designed by Thomas Hamilton in 1825-9, as part of the Greek Revival of the north.

READY-MADE NEOCLASSICAL RUINS

For all the high-mindedness shown by European Neoclassicists at this time, with their volumes of learned essays and sheaves of detailed drawings, many of them, no matter what their nationality, were in some way seduced by the romantic aspects of the ancient ruins. This was made evident by the predilection of many otherwise highly rational architects for producing designs of ruined structures, which appeared to already have succumbed to the ravages of time. The most extreme example of such a ready-made ruin was Clérisseau's famous drawing of a ruined room at Trinità dei Monti in Rome.

Classical public buildings were not only being designed in Britain and France. Towards the end of the Neoclassical period, as the influence of the second generation of French architects made itself felt, great urban structures grew up elsewhere in Europe, particularly in Germany.

NEOCLASSICAL BERLIN

Germany was still, at this time, a grouping of monarchical states. Berlin was the centre of Prussia, and its ruler, Friedrich Wilhelm III (1770–1840), lived in the small palace in the heart of the city. An enlightened monarch interested in the arts, he had travelled extensively—to Rome, Naples, even to St Petersburg—and he was anxious to use what he had seen in Berlin. Architecturally, Berlin was a rather dull city at the end of the eighteenth century. Long, straight streets bordered by flat-fronted uniform houses gave little variety to the scene.

But then, in the 1790s, there seemed to emerge an unplanned movement, spearheaded by a group of innovative architects who together changed the face of Berlin. There was David Gilly who in 1793 founded a school of architecture (which became the Academy in 1799) among whose pupils were both his son Friedrich (1772–1800) and Karl Friedrich Schinkel (1781–1841), later hailed as one of Germany's greatest Neoclassical architects. There was also Carl Langhans (1732–1808), who came to Berlin as Director of the Royal Office of Public Buildings. Between 1788 and 1791 he designed the Brandenburg Gate, an imposing monument surrounded by two colonnaded wings. And finally there was Gottfried Schadow, who spent three years in Rome and then returned to Berlin in 1787 to become the director of Royal Sculpture Commissions and later director of the Akademie der Kunste.

Another who had travelled extensively in Italy was Heinrich Gentz (1766–1811), one of Berlin's leading state architects. Gentz had spent four years in Sicily and also visited Paestum and Rome, where there was then a large German-speaking circle, including Goethe and the painter Angelica Kauffmann. On returning to Berlin in 1795, he was appointed Inspector of Royal Buildings.

The west side of Charlotte Square,
Edinburgh, with a central church, and
five or six houses on the side.

Karl Friedrich Schinkel (1781–1841),
the Prussian architect, thought of by
some as the greatest German architect of
the nineteenth century, and the founder of
German Neoclassicism.

SCHINKEL, GERMANY'S PREMIER NEOCLASSICAL ARCHITECT

In a small city, any group of artists will live and work closely together. Berlin was no exception. Gentz, for example, married Friedrich Gilly's sister, and taught at Gilly's Bauakademie from 1798, where he introduced Neoclassicism with a Greek flavour to Berlin. At this time he met the young Karl Friedrich Schinkel, the name most often associated with Neoclassical architecture in Germany. Working towards the end of the fruitful Neoclassical period, the Prussian-born Schinkel was educated in Berlin and spent time in both Italy and Paris early in the nineteenth century. He was not so much interested in the archaeological aspect of antiquities, but in the original buildings he viewed. Back in Germany, Schinkel first worked as a painter and theatrical designer.

Napoleon's entry into Berlin effectively stopped any sort of building until 1815, the conclusion of the Napoleonic wars, and so Schinkel did not begin to practise as an architect until then, when Friedrich Wilhelm III commissioned him to design a new royal guardhouse in Unter den Linden, the Neue Wache. Then in 1818 came the Schauspielhaus theatre and concert house. Both guardhouse and theatre were classically inspired, the latter in particular based on several examples of memorable Greek architecture, including the Choragic Monument of Lysicrates in Athens. The Altes Museum followed in 1823, an imposing building with a long façade of Ionic columns, and then later still the new Bauakademie, or school of architecture. The face of Berlin had been irrevocably changed. Many more buildings were envisaged and planned, but several schemes never came to fruition.

KARLSRUHE: A NEW TOWN
Freidrich Weinbrenner (1766–1826), who was born in Karlsruhe, went first to Berlin, where he met both Langhans and Gilly, and then to Rome to study antiquities. He returned to Karlsruhe in 1797 and worked there in the Neoclassical idiom, building new public squares and streets between 1804 and 1824—so many of them, in fact, that Karlsruhe is spoken of in the same breath as Edinburgh as a New Town. Not surprisingly, Weinbrenner was named Director of Public Buildings in Karlsruhe, and he also established a school of architecture there.

KLENZE AND LUDWIG IN BAVARIA
Although they were separate states, there was artistic and academic communication between Prussia and Bavaria. Munich, then the capital of Bavaria, came to embrace Neoclassicism at much the same time as Prussia. It was lucky in its architects. Leo von Klenze (1784–1864) studied in Berlin under Gilly and with Percier and Fontaine in Paris, and in 1816 became architect to the Crown Prince Ludwig, who lived in Munich and became King Ludwig I in 1825. One of Klenze's first commissions for Ludwig was the Glyptothek—the Greek word for sculpture hall—built to house Ludwig's collection of antiquities, which included the Aegina Marbles. Notable for being the first ever public sculpture gallery, Klenze's design was in a suitably Antique style: a veritable Temple of Sculpture. Then followed the picture gallery, Pinakothek (1822–25), and eventually, on the Königsplatz, a purely Greek Propylaeum, first proposed in 1817 but not built until 1846–60. With its distinctive wings, the Propylaeum looked much like its Athenian inspiration, the imposing gateway to the Acropolis.

Ludwig's wish was to enrich his capital with buildings of beauty, and many of his other commissions reflected his Neoclassical leanings in architecture. Karl von Fischer (1782–1820), for example, who trained in Munich and Vienna, was asked to design a new urban layout for Munich and provided various architectural schemes for the Prussian monarch, including the National Theatre (1811–18), a Neoclassical but conventional structure.

The Walhalla, a monumental temple that Ludwig wanted to build, was the subject of designs from both Fischer and Klenze. That of the latter was preferred, and the huge structure (1830–42) was built near Regensburg as one of the latest and most Grecian of all the German Greek Revival buildings.

The Befreiungshalle, near Kelheim, first designed by Friedrich von Garner, and then redesigned by Leo von Klenze in 1842 to commemorate the war of Liberation against Napoleon.

The Walhalla, Leo von Klenze's massive Greek-style commemorative temple, built near Regensburg in 1830–42.

One of the most dramatic of monuments that Klenze worked on was the Befrieungshalle or Hall of Liberation built in 1842, near Kelheim. This enormous rotunda, designed to commemorate the War of Liberation against Napleon which took place between 1813 and 1815, was first conceived by Friedrich von Gartner, who also worked for Ludwig I, often in competition with Klenze. After Gartner's death in 1847, the Befrieungshalle was remodelled by Klenze in stark, almost bleak style.

Neoclassicism was not just found in the cosmopolitan capitals of Europe. Throughout the period and all over the continent, churches and castles were designed in the Neoclassical style, as in Hungary, where a European baroque style was replaced, in part, by one with more classical

overtones. Both the early Vac Cathedral (1767–72) and the later Esztergom Cathedral (1822–50) drew heavily on classical references.

Vac Cathedral was designed by Isidore Canevale, and with its impressive and immense portico was remarkable for its time. Esztergom was built nearly a hundred years later by J. S. Pack and Joszef Hild, the latter also designing the cathedral at Eger.

Michael Johann Pollak (1773–1855) was possibly the leading Hungarian classicist. Coming from a family of architects—both his father and step-brother practised the art—he studied in Milan, and returned to Budapest in 1798. There he designed the Theatre and Assembly Room, both with strong classical overtones, and the National Museum.

Gloriette in Schonbrunn Park, designed by Ferdinand von Hohenburg in 1775 showing the peculiarly European architecture that emerged during the transition from the Baroque to Neoclassicism.

The tomb of Archduchess Marie Christine in the Augustinian Church in Vienna, one of the greatest Neoclassical monuments, combining Egyptian as well as Greek and Roman elements. It was sculpted by Antonio Canova between 1799 and 1805.

The bathroom at Schloss Wilhelmshohe, near Kassel, built by Simon-Louis Ry. He was the fourth generation of his family to practise architecture, and studied with the great Neoclassical theorist Blondel in Paris before travelling to Italy.

*Colonnade at Kacina Castle, Sedlec, in
Czechoslovakia, 1802–22.*

*The Roman-style interior of the
Cathedral at Eger in Hungary, designed
by Joszef Hild.*

RUSSIA'S GOLDEN AGE

Neoclassicism in Russia began during the time of Peter the Great, whose wide and varied interests included Western architecture, but the style did not mature until the reign of his successor, Catherine the Great.

Peter the Great was a human dynamo, a man of great energy and ambition. Determined to have a capital and port that matched any in the Western world, he decided to build a city in the decidedly unpromising marshlands on the banks of the Neva River, facing the Gulf of Finland. To this end, bending towards Europe, he imported European ideas and architects, like the Frenchman Jean-Baptiste Le Blond (1679–1719), who went to the new St Petersburg in 1715.

The Tsar ordered Le Blond to design a country palace for him outside St Petersburg, on a site overlooking the sea where he could watch his fleet on manoeuvres in the Gulf. Although much altered by Rastrelli later in the

The palace at Peterhof near St Petersburg, built for Peter the Great, then enlarged and rebuilt during Elizabeth's reign by the Italian Neoclassical architect B. F. Rastrelli. It was further added to during Catherine's reign.

Catherine the Great of Russia. She reigned from 1762—96, and in that time commissioned the greatest European designers to produce art of all descriptions, from ceramics to furniture and paintings to palaces, amassing an unrivalled collection.

century, Peterhof Palace was one of the earliest Neoclassical buildings in Russia.

A generation later Jean-Baptiste Vallin de le Mothe (1729–1800), amongst others, was invited to Russia in 1759 by Count Ivan Shuvalov, a cousin and pupil of the influential French Architect Jean-François Blondel, to construct the Academy of Fine Arts in St Petersburg (which had been designed by Blondel).

Russian architects were studying and working with their French counterparts in Paris by the middle of the eighteenth century. This was a fecund period that coincided with the accession to the throne, after a coup, of Catherine II—Catherine the Great—in 1762. She turned to architecture with a passion, determined to make Russia as famous for its buildings as France or England. In 1779 she asked the Italian Giacomo Quarenghi (1744–1817) to work for her, and in the 1780s Quarenghi designed both the Academy of Sciences and the Hermitage Theatre in St Petersburg, as well as the English Palace at Peterhof. His Alexander Palace at Tsarskoe Selo was built during the next decade, as were the Smolny Institute and the Riding School, both in St Petersburg.

Also in St Petersburg, Ivan Starov (1783–1808), who had studied in Paris with de Wailly in the 1760s, designed the Tauride Palace (1743–88) for Potemkin, and Andrei Voronikhin (1760–1814), built the Cathedral of the Virgin of Kazan (1801–11) and the Paestum-inspired Academy of Mines (1806–11).

But it was not until the reign of Alexander I that full-blooded Neoclassicism came to Russia. During his rule Thomas de Thomon (1754–1813), Architect in Chief to the Admiralty, built the Bourse at St Petersburg (1804–10), and Russian-born Adrian Dmitrievich Zakharov designed the Admiralty (1806–15).

The Grand Imperial theatre, St Petersburg (Leningrad), painted by B. Paterssen in 1806. The city was the product of the westernizing zeal of both Peter the Great and Catherine the Great.

SCANDINAVIAN NEOCLASSICISM

Neoclassical architecture altered in every country, often in accordance with native styles and traditions. Sometimes it was heavier, sometimes simpler; sometimes classically correct, at other times merely touched by the Antique. Scandinavia was no exception, and had its own particular brand of Neoclassicism.

In Sweden Neoclassical design was much influenced by Jean-Louis Desprez (1743–1804). Born in France, in 1776 he went as a Grand Prix winner to Rome, where he studied architecture and painting. He became a stage designer, but was then hired by Gustav III of Sweden in 1784, and he lived in that country until his death, working as an architect. His Botanicum at Uppsala (1788) was an early and influential example of the Grecian Revival.

There was French influence in Denmark, too, through Nicolas-Henri Jardin (1720–99) who came to Denmark in 1755, where he taught at the Royal Academy. One of his pupils was Casper Frederick Harsdorff (1735–99), who later studied under Blondel in Paris, after winning a travel bursary allowing him to spend six years in Paris and Rome. On his return Harsdorff, who became Royal Inspector of Buildings in 1770, designed,

among other things, the Moltke Chapel at Karise (1761–66) and the cool and beautiful mortuary Chapel of Frederik V in Roskilde cathedral (designed 1768–78 and completed 1821–25, after Harsdorff's death, by Christian Frederik Hansen).

The Copenhagen-born Hansen (1756–1845) studied in the Danish capital before going to Italy, where he stayed until 1784. His work in Copenhagen, like the group of law courts and prison (1803–16), and the Church of Our Lady, or Vor Frue Kirke (1811–29), showed a solid simplicity of design.

Until 1809 Finland was ruled by Sweden and afterwards became a Grand Duchy of Russia. It benefited considerably from its cosmopolitan history. With the advent of the Russians, the capital was moved from Turku to Helsinki, and Carl Ludwig Engel (1778–1840) was appointed architect in charge of the city's reconstruction. Although working in Russia prior to this, Engel was born in Berlin, had studied at the Bauakadamie under Friedrich Gilly and was a contemporary of Schinkel. He designed several fine Neoclassical buildings for the new capital (and outside Helsinki as well), including the naval barracks on Katajanokka peninsula and the imposing Bock House.

The foyer of Drottningholm Court Theatre, near Stockholm, designed for Gustav III of Sweden in the Neoclassical style.

THE NEW WORLD AND JEFFERSON

Across the Atlantic, the young America was proceeding architecturally, as with everything else at that time, in a different direction from the Old World.

Public architecture was initially low down the early settlers' priorities, but the time came when an official State building was needed in one of the oldest colonial settlements, Virginia. Thomas Jefferson (1743–1826) had been sent to Paris in 1784, as America's Minister to France, and he was known as a man of wide artistic interests, including architecture, then a virtually unknown discipline in the United States. It was Jefferson who said: 'Architecture is my delight and putting up, and pulling down, one of my favorite amusements.'

Not surprisingly, the Virginian elders appealed to their most cultured of native sons for a suitable design for their new State Capitol. A disciple of Palladio even before his stay in France, Jefferson had travelled extensively through Europe, some of the time with the ubiquitous Clérisseau. He was delighted at seeing first-hand the remains of the classical world and at Nîmes he stopped in wonder by the Maison Carrée (16 BC), gazing at it, as he said in a letter to James Madison, 'for whole hours, like a lover at his mistress.' Naturally, he recommended to his fellow Virginians that this imposing Roman temple would make a perfect model for the new State Capitol. He wrote to his friend Clérisseau, who had made drawings of the Maison and other antiquities at Nîmes, asking him to make a stucco model, but to change the order from Corinthian to Ionic, the latter considered by Jefferson more suitable for a Capitol. His plan was nearly quashed, however, for work started before Clérisseau's designs were received; but several furious letters later, he persuaded the politicians to revert to his scheme, saying, 'it will give unrivalled honour to our state and furnish a model whereon to form the taste of our young men'. Completed in 1796, with the help of Benjamin Latrobe, the Virginia State Capitol did indeed prove an inspired role model for future such state structures.

Jefferson also worked with the French architect and engineer, Pierre L'Enfant, on plans for the nation's new capital of Washington. He gave the Frenchman city plans of places like Paris and Karlsruhe, which he collected during his time in France, again stressing that he thought some structures should be based on 'models of antiquity'. At his suggestion, a competition for the designs of the new Presidential Residence and the Capitol was held in 1792, the former being won by James Hoban, the latter by William Thornton (this last also a saga of feuds and arguments).

Jefferson's most ambitious architectural creation was the University of Virginia at Charlottesville (1817–26), which was to be 'an academical village' of several smallish buildings arranged around a square. When finished, the university had ten pavilions based on monuments like the Theatre of Marcellus, the Baths of Diocletian and the Temple of Trajan, all buildings of Antiquity that Jefferson loved. Even the library was inspired by the Pantheon at Rome.

The Rotunda, which contains a circular library, and some of the classical Pavilions of the University of Virginia at Charlottesville, designed by Thomas Jefferson.

OTHER AMERICAN NEOCLASSICISTS

This enthusiasm for the classic influenced many more early American buildings, based as they were on a rather amateur enthusiasm for Antiquity, as well as on the Palladian and Greek influences emanating from Europe.

Boston-born Charles Bulfinch (1763–1844) toured Europe in the 1780s, returning to his home town to practise as an amateur architect. He submitted the winning design for the new Massachusetts State House, which was built on top of Beacon Hill (1793–1820), and indeed much of Boston's town planning resulted from Bulfinch's classical enthusiasm.

The other major American architect working at that time was the aforementioned Benjamin Latrobe (1764–1820), who was born in Yorkshire and educated in Germany (his mother was German). He returned to England to become a pupil of S. P. Cockerell, and was much influenced by the work of John Soane. Latrobe emigrated to the United States in 1796, becoming one of the first new American architects to have genuine European experience and knowledge. In 1795 he aided Jefferson with the Virginia Capitol, three years later he designed Philadelphia's Bank of Pennsylvania in a forward-looking classical style, and in 1803 he went to Washington to work on the Capitol. The construction of the Capitol was still dominated by competition-winner William Thornton, who had so far collaborated unsuccessfully with Stephen Hallet, his French runner-up in the contest, and George Hadfield, an Englishman. Latrobe worked closely with Thornton, changing the internal design of the structure and inventing a new order to add to the classical five—the 'American Order,' wherein the acanthus leaves were replaced by corn leaves. The completed Capitol burned down in 1814, and this time Latrobe was able to rebuild the whole complex on his own, until Thornton's continuing criticisms led to his

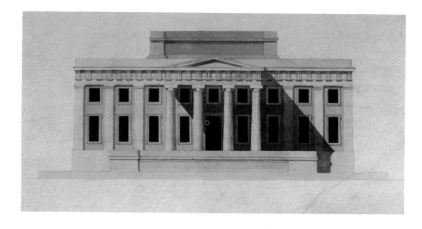

resignation in 1817. He then went to help Jefferson with his designs for the University of Virginia.

Latrobe's two pupils, William Strickland (1788–1854) and Robert Mills (1781–1855), continued their mentor's classically based work well into the nineteenth century. Strickland's Bank of the United States in Philadelphia (now the Customs House), built from 1818 to 1824, was closely modelled on the Parthenon, and his Tennessee State Capitol at Nashville, built as late as 1845, is porticoed and towered. Robert Mills built both churches and public buildings in a Greek Revival manner, and his adherence to Neoclassicism allowed him to build the Doric-column Washington Monument at Baltimore (1814–29) and the Washington Monument obelisk in Washington, D.C., not completed until 1884.

Above: *A design for a State Capitol by the American architect, Thomas Ustick Walter, born in Philadelphia. Amongst other projects he worked on the completion of the Capitol in Washington, from 1851.*

Federal houses in Georgetown, Washington DC, showing how the same elements of a broad Neoclassical style could be interpreted in different - in this case, simpler - ways by different countries.

The Capitol, Washington DC, the final result of the ideas and designs of so many people, including Jefferson, Latrobe, Stephen Hallet, Thornton, Walter and, latterly, Bulfinch, who was in charge of work on the building between 1817 and 1830.

IV

THE NEOCLASSICAL HOUSE

L AVISH DOMESTIC HOUSES ARE the products of a time of peace. The villa, the ultimate domestic dwelling, evolved from the relatively simple houses of Ancient Greece into sophisticated structures in the Roman Empire that ranged from a landowner's rambling house set in the centre of his domain to a refined city dwelling.

From Roman times, villas were always the prerogative of the newly landed middle classes. Eventually, as the energy of Imperial Rome slowly sapped away, rich Romans were to be far more concerned with building and embellishing their villas than furthering the glory of the Empire.

COUNTRY SEATS IN THE ROMAN EMPIRE

By the time Pompeii was built, the house or villa in Rome was well established; it extended to a complicated and sophisticated dwelling with a system of interconnecting rooms, including servants' quarters that did not

Grange Park, Hampshire, designed by William Wilkins, architect of the National Gallery, in 1809. The dramatic temple-like structure was based on several different Greek monuments, and was seen as the embodiment of the nineteenth-century Greek Revival.

intrude on those of the masters. The Roman owners took as much care with the design of their houses as the most particular of eighteenth-century earls. Country houses particularly were often very large, and very well organized. Pliny the younger had one on Laurentium, about 27 kilometres from Rome, which he cared for passionately. Of it, he wrote:

> You may wonder why my Laurentine place is such a joy to me, but once you realize the attractions of the house itself, the amenities of its situation, and its extensive sea front, you will have your answer.
>
> The house is large enough for my needs, but not expensive to keep up. It opens into a hall, unpretentious but not without dignity, and then there are two colonnades, rounded like the letter D, which enclose a small but pleasant courtyard. This makes a splendid retreat in bad weather, being protected by windows and still more by the overhanging roof. Opposite the middle of it is a cheerful inner hall, and then a dining room which is really rather fine: it runs out towards the shore, and whenever the sea is driven inland by the south-west wind it is lightly washed by the spray of the spent breakers. It has folding doors and windows as large as the doors all round, so that at the front and sides it seems to look out on to three seas, and at the back has a view through the inner hall, the courtyard with the two colonnades, and the entrance hall to the woods and the mountains in the distance.

The barbarous times that followed the Roman Empire signalled the end of large unfortified domestic dwellings, and it was not until the coming of the Renaissance that people were once again able to think about building for peaceful lives.

RAPID HOUSE-BUILDING IN THE 1700S

By 1700, many more people had money than a hundred years before. Landowners were prosperous and those who were making money in commerce or finance bought land, both as an investment and as a way of entering society. Celia Fiennes noted with pleasure the amount of new building going on—and was dismissive of those old houses still standing. Of Wolseley Hall, Staffordshire, the home of her aunt, she disparagingly said that 'the best roomes were newer built with chambers over them and a very good staircase well wanscoated and carv'd with good pictures; the rest of the house is all old and low and must be new built'.

And 'new built' they were, in a surge of building that continued for the next fifty years. The number of houses in London grew enormously, altering the city forever. In 1776, Horace Walpole wrote: 'So great is the rage of building everywhere, that, if I stay here a fortnight, without going to town, I look about to see if no new house is built since I went last.'

The styles employed were of course various, but it would not be an exaggeration to say that most of those early houses built in the new Neoclassical style were based on the work and designs of the sixteenth-century architect, Andrea Palladio, even today one of the best known and most influential architects of all time.

THE INFLUENCE OF PALLADIO

Andrea Palladio (1508–80) was born in Padua, a child of the Renaissance. He started work in Vicenza, where he met his patron, Count Giangiorgio Trissino, who in 1545 took him to Rome for two years to study antiquities. When he returned he worked in Vicenza for a time, but soon found himself undertaking more and more commissions to build country houses in the Veneto for the rich and independent Venetians. Between 1547 and 1570, he built eleven such villas, as well as other, more public works. The typical Palladian Venetian villa was designed with a relatively compact central living block, with wings on each side that either extended in a straight line or curved around. He published several important books, including *Le Antichità di Roma* in 1554 and his most influential—the book that, in a sense, spawned the whole Neoclassical movement—*I Quattro Libri dell'architettura* in 1570.

The frontispiece of I Quattro Libri dell'architettura *by Andrea Palladio. First published in Venice in 1570, it was published in English between 1715–1720 by Giacomo Leoni. The Earl of Burlington was amongst its subscribers.*

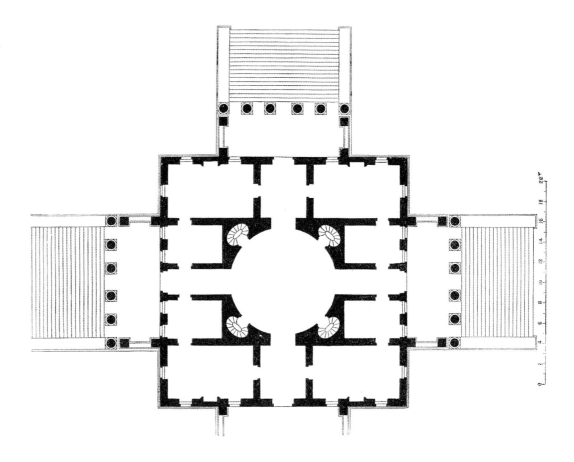

The plans and façade of Andrea Palladio's Villa Rotonda, later known as Villa Capra, at Vicenza. It was commissioned by Paolo Almerico in 1566 and was later sold to the Capra family. It served as a model for countless houses two hundred years later.

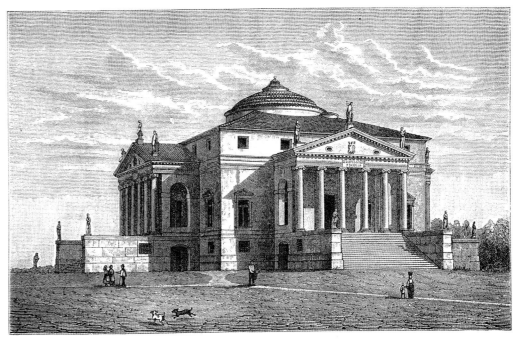

Although he was a fervent disciple of Vitruvius, Palladio's designs were not, as was sometimes thought at the time, exact reproductions of the villas of the Ancients. He took as his principles Ancient ideas, as described by Vitruvius, and altered them to produce what, in his mind, was the perfect dwelling for his clients, the Venetian landed gentry.

And so it continued. Palladio in the sixteenth century, Palladian disciples in the eighteenth century. The era was different, but the aims were the same: a simple but solid dwelling that showed the world that here dwelt a man secure and content. It was a style that implied wealth and leisure.

NEOCLASSICISM MEETS THE ENGLISH COUNTRY HOUSE

It would be no exaggeration to say that during the 1700s the English became the masters of the country house; in fact, English Neoclassicism was personified by it. In France and Germany houses were either of the rambling farmhouse type, or small châteaux or *Schlösser*. In France the aristocracy was supposed to spend most of its time at court, not, as in England, on its estates. Only in England, and later in America, did there emerge the smallish self-contained, and specially designed, family house. This size house suited not only the new English landed class—and they were there in increasing numbers—but also the traditional English gentleman. The apparent simplicity of Palladio's designs was much taken to heart.

At the beginning of the eighteenth century, architecture was an art which could be studied and practised by all. Great interest was taken in the design of a house: one's own, one's neighbours', even those of people one did not know at all. It was considered perfectly normal, not to say correct, to visit the local gentlemen's houses should one be in the district, even if no acquaintance of the gentlemen had ever been made. The casual visitor expected permission to walk in the grounds and through the house, admiring and criticizing as he saw fit.

OPEN HOUSES AND UNINVITED VISITORS

From Horace Walpole to Alexander Pope, including men and women of far lesser talents, many wrote down their views on what they saw. Walpole did not only write about the houses he viewed, he suffered the same 'unexpected visitors' experience himself. On returning in 1761 to his father's house, Houghton (which had been decorated by Kent), he was caught unawares by a visiting party:

> A party arrived, just as I did, to see the house, a man and three women in riding dresses, and they rode post through the apartments. I could not hurry before them fast enough; they were not so long in seeing for the first time, as I could have been in one room, to examine what I knew by heart. I remember formerly being often diverted with this kind of seers; they come, ask what such a room is called, in which Sir Robert lay, write it down, admire a lobster or a cabbage in a marketpiece, dispute whether

the last room was green or purple, and then hurry to the inn for fear the fish should be over-dressed.

The practice continued into the nineteenth century. For instance, in 1820 the gardener and architect John Claudius Loudon wrote, after one of his exhaustive tours, about the house of the unsuspecting Mr Mangles, near Sunning Hill. Remarking that he has noticed before that it is very 'highly kept', he goes on to enumerate the housekeeping arrangements, noting:

> Mr Mangles' dressing-room and business-room. Clothes-press admirably arranged; the drawers containing the different parts of dress, named and numbered. Complete system of housekeeping books; letters and copying machine; engraved forms of bankers' checks; with the family arms, view of the house, &c.

Woe betide those with something to hide.

INIGO JONES, FATHER OF ENGLISH NEOCLASSICISM

Inigo Jones (1573–1652), the great seventeenth-century architect, was the father of the English Neoclassical movement. He made at least two visits to Italy, one around 1613 with the early collector of antiquities, the Earl of Arundel. On that trip he would have seen not only Renaissance architecture and Palladio's work in the villas of the Veneto, but also every monument that was visible. On his return in 1618, he was commissioned to build, at Greenwich, a new house for Queen Anne of Denmark, the wife of James I. The Queen's House took a leisurely twenty years to complete, and incorporated, for the first time in England, the Palladian principles that Jones had absorbed. Although Roger Pratt (1620–84), working some years after Jones, continued in the classical vein, little of any note was designed along such lines until a hundred years later.

COLEN CAMPBELL AND *VITRUVIUS BRITANNICUS*

In about 1715, a hitherto little-known Scottish architect named Colen Campbell published the first volume of his work, *Vitruvius Britannicus*. As might have been expected from the title, this was not a translation of the works of the Roman architect, but rather a new collection of classical designs for houses by both Campbell and other contemporary architects, showing detailed plans and elevations. Not surprisingly, his own work figured prominently, such as Mereworth Castle (1722–25), which he built for the Earl of Westmoreland and which is modelled closely on Villa Rotonda at Vicenza. One of the travelling commentators of the time, William Hugh Dalton, writing around 1796, much approved of this seat:

> The ancient structure [a castle belonging to the Nevils, Lords of Abergavenny] having been pulled down, Mr Campbell, the architect, built another from one of the designs of Palladio, in imitation of a grand palace in Florence. It is moated round to complete the original design; and near the house is a rising

Interior of the Queen's House, Greenwich, by Inigo Jones. This perfectly executed Palladian villa by the Thames (c 1640) underlines Jones' position as the father of English classicism—and expresses the coolness and clarity which characterized English Neoclassicism of a century later.

ground, from which there is a most extensive and beautiful prospect.

Dalton was not quite so admiring about the most famous structure Campbell designed, the large and imposing Wanstead House. This was built for Robert Child, the banker, between 1713 and 1720, and figured prominently in *Vitruvius Britannicus*. Travelling in the district some years later, Dalton said of it:

> It is reckoned, both for building and gardens, one of the most elegant houses in England; it is constructed according to the best rules in the Corinthian order, and the front entirely of Portland stone; the portico in the centre is supported by pillars of the Corinthian order and under it is the landing place that leads to the great hall, where there is a vast variety of ornaments and paintings by the best masters in Italy.... Mr Campbell, the author of *Vitruvius Britannicus*, was the architect employed in contriving this noble house, or rather palace; and although in particular parts, it has beauties exceeding many of the best houses in the kingdom, yet, when all the parts are taken together, it seems to want some of that proportion necessary to set off the whole. The abilities of the architect are very well known, but possibly he might be, as he was on many other occasions, crossed in his design.

Despite Dalton's reservations, Wanstead was hugely influential on the direction of Neoclassical design over the next twenty years. Campbell himself went on to build many more Palladian-inspired houses in Britain over the next two decades, and these and his volumes of *Vitruvius Britannicus* meant that the Palladian ideal was widely disseminated.

WILLIAM ADAM AND SCOTTISH NEOCLASSICISM

Another Scotsman, William Adam (1689–1748), was, by the 1720s, very busy indeed. As well as his public buildings, the father of Robert and James worked on most of the great houses of Scotland between 1720 and 1740, either altering, extending or building them from scratch. Scottish nobles undertook the Grand Tour with as much enthusiasm as their English cousins and by 1720 were anxious to give classical tone to their houses, particularly since several of them were importing Antique works, classical marbles and casts. By the time of his death, he had worked for, among others, the Earls of Hopetoun, Stair, Bute, Findlater, Ilay and Hay; the Dukes of Roxburghe, Argyll and Hamilton, and the Marquis of Tweeddale. Adam's designs were classically simple in the Palladian tradition, and owed nothing to Greek revival. That was to come.

Farther south, other houses in the new style were being built as well, with architects like James Gibbs, of St Martin-in-the-Fields fame, building Ditchley House (1720), for which the busy William Kent painted one of his famous ceilings.

Lord Burlington subscribed to *Vitruvius Britannicus*, and in 1721 he commissioned Colen Campbell to complete the reconstruction of his residence in Piccadilly, Burlington House, taking over from James Gibbs.

Aerial view of Mereworth Castle in Kent. Colen Campbell modelled the house closely on Palladio's Villa Rotonda.

BURLINGTON AND KENT

The Earl of Burlington came into his inheritance when he was only nine, and by the time he was 21 he had already visited Italy once to see the classical remains. It was on his second trip, four years later in 1719, that he met William Kent (1685–1748), who was then a painter working in Rome. They returned to London together, and until the end of Kent's life worked in tandem on architectural plans.

Chiswick House (1725–29) was the first project that Lord Burlington and William Kent worked on together. Built when the original house was still standing, it was in the Palladian style, loosely modelled on the Villa Rotonda. In the grounds Burlington added a miniature, or casino. Casinos, which were very fashionable in the eighteenth century, did not have the connotation they have today. The word meant simply 'little house,' and it generally implied an ornamental house in the grounds of a larger house, often used to accommodate gentlemen's Grand Tour collections.

Richard Burlington designed some serious projects, such as the Assembly Rooms at York, but he also designed small buildings, playthings of a sort, for his friends. At Charleton, in Sussex he built one of the 'many small houses built by persons of quality who used to reside there during the season for fox-hunting. The most beautiful of these houses is that erected by his grace, the late Duke of Richmond. It is a large room, called Fox-Hall, designed by the Earl of Burlington, where the gentlemen dine together every day during their stay at Charleton.'

After meeting Lord Burlington in Rome in 1719, Kent was to work with him in England on every aspect of houses and gardens until his death in 1748. Horace Walpole, never short of a succinct word or two, summed up his career: 'He was a painter and architect and the father of modern gardening. In the first character he was below mediocrity; in the second he was a restorer of the science; in the last, an original, and the inventor of an art that realizes painting, and improves nature.'

Kent began his professional life not as an architect but as a painter, being sent to Italy at the age of 24 by some Yorkshire gentlemen who raised a sum for his expenses. He stayed there for ten years, until he met Lord Burlington. Back in London and with an apartment in Burlington House, Kent worked first as a portrait painter.

Luckily, Kent then started to work with Burlington on architectural projects, and because of his 'excellent taste for ornaments', he was soon in great demand. It was not until at least 1730 that he did any major architectural work, that project being Holkham Hall, on which he worked with Burlington and its owner, Thomas Coke, the Earl of Leicester. Kent's taste in interiors was rich and lavish, and he enjoyed much popularity among the smart London set, even designing architectural evening dresses for two fashionable ladies: 'The one he dressed in a petticoat decorated with columns of the five orders; the other like a bronze, in a copper coloured sattin with ornaments of gold.' Some of Kent's best work was at Rousham in Oxfordshire, where he improved the old house and added a library.

Holkham Hall, in Norfolk, was one of the greatest of the early Palladian houses. The Earl of Leicester's interest in architecture, combined with the talents of Burlington and Kent, made it unique. Coke (a member of the Society of Dilettanti), Burlington and Kent formulated its design, based on

Chiswick House, the villa belonging to, and designed by, the Earl of Burlington with the help of William Kent, in 1729. Like Mereworth, it was heavily influenced by the Villa Rotonda.

Holkham Hall in north Norfolk, the imposing seat of Thomas Coke, Earl of Leicester. Designed by him, in conjunction with Burlington and Kent, the plans were executed by Matthew Brettingham. The house was much admired in its day.

various aspects of Palladian villas, and Matthew Brettingham drew up and executed the plans. Celebrated in its own time, it was built on a grand scale, with a long frontage and a triumphal arch.

Matthew Brettingham (1699–1769) was yet another early exponent of Palladianism. He spent some time in Rome buying antiquities for the Earl of Leicester, and after Holkham Hall, he began designing Kedleston, in Derbyshire, the home of Sir Nathaniel Curzon, which was later worked on by James Paine, with Robert Adam in control of the interior.

James Paine (1717–89), too, continued the Palladian tradition in the Midlands and the North of England. Nostell Priory was designed by him, and he was the architect for Kedleston, responsible for both its Greek Hall and its dome of Ancients, 'proportioned chiefly from the Pantheon at Rome and Spalatro'.

NEOCLASSICISM'S NEW WAVE

With the deaths of William Kent in 1748 and Lord Burlington in 1753, the first, overwhelmingly Palladian phase of English Neoclassicism was over. But William Chambers returned from Rome in 1755, Robert Adam returned in 1758 and George III came to the throne in 1760. The time was ripe for something new, and a second wave of Neoclassicism took hold.

Although William Chambers spent much of his time on official architectural commissions, he did build villas and houses. In particular, there were the little Casino at Marino and Charlemont House in Dublin, both for Lord Charlemont (the latter considered the first truly Neoclassical house in the Irish city). Chambers also was responsible for Lord Bessborough's semi-Palladian villa at Roehampton (now a school), and Peper Harow for Lord Middleton in Surrey, both well thought of in their day.

The porch of Chandos House, designed by Robert Adam in the early 1770s for the third Duke of Chandos. He designed several other great London houses in this period, including 20 St James's Square, and Derby House.

THE EXEMPLARY BROTHERS ADAM

Chambers' rival, Robert Adam, was also working in England at the same time. After he came back from Italy, he was determined to build up his practice as quickly as possible. Indeed, Adam's work stood out among that of his contemporaries. He combined the maturity of classical art and architecture with a contemporary feeling that owed a little to the light touch of the rococo, a bit to the composition of Raphael and a great deal to his own perception that tone and texture carried as much weight as accurate measurements.

Both Robert and his younger brother James Adam (1732–94) always stressed that in the matter of translating Ancient style into contemporary design, it was they who were correct, and others who had it wrong. The early classicists, they said, used the vocabulary of temple and forum, as seen through the eyes of Palladio; it amounted to a monumental style that was neither suitable nor correct for the design of houses. The Adams, on the other hand, drew on the domestic buildings of Ancient Rome, using what they had learned and seen of villas that had been excavated.

The Adam brothers were not alone in their view of the suitability of temples as architectural models. The venerable and influential Jean-François Blondel, in the first volume of *Cours d'architecture*, had also asked why people should use Greek forms, when such were only employed in temples and rarely employed for decorative domestic use.

Be that as it may, there was no doubt that the view Robert Adam brought to Neoclassicism was completely different from that which had gone before. His experience throughout Europe—in Spalatro as well as Rome and Naples—gave him a confidence in the style, and a breadth and

ability to mix classical reference and allusion in a way that had not been done before—and which is shown at its purest in the interiors he did for so many houses.

Although Robert Adam designed the new garden front at Kedleston, as he did the portico at Osterley Park and some complete houses, notably 20 St James's Square and 20 Portman Square, both in London, on the whole his best and the majority of his work comprised the drastic remodelling and rebuilding of existing houses, as at Syon and Kedleston. He changed Syon from an inconvenient, old-fashioned place into a dwelling where there existed, according to John Soane, 'the Taste and Magnificence of a Roman Villa, with all the comforts and conveniences of an English Nobleman's residence'.

The garden front of Kedleston Hall in Derbyshire, home of Lord Scarsdale. It was designed by Robert Adam, as were many of the interiors, adding to the original designs by Brettingham and Paine.

The pediment screen at Osterley Park House in Middlesex, designed by Robert Adam around 1760 as an addition to the existing house.

OTHER NOTABLE BRITISH ARCHITECTS

Like French architects before them, this new generation of young English architects had, almost to a man, been to Rome. George Dance the younger and his artist brother Nathaniel were there at the end of the 1750s, as were Scotsman Robert Mylne, James Wyatt and, a little later on, John Soane. The only one of the group who did not go was Henry Holland.

George Dance probably concentrated more on public buildings, but over a working life of more than forty years, he did build some houses, including the influential Cranbury Park and Stratton Park, which, with its Doric portico, was an early indication of the Greek Revival to come.

James Wyatt (1747–1813), another Italian-influenced architect, worked in several styles, not simply the Neoclassical (see p. 65). In the domestic sphere, he designed several classical houses, notably Heveningham Hall, after the death of the original architect, and Dodington in Gloucestershire, an example of Greek revivalism built for Christopher Codrington.

Henry Holland (see p. 63) gained the commission to rebuild the old Carlton House for the Prince of Wales, which he did in 1783, and found thereafter that commissions followed thick and fast. He worked at Althorp, Woburn and Brighton, on the house that eventually was to become the Prince Regent's Pavilion.

Apsley House, known colloquially as 'No. 1, London', designed by the brothers Adam around 1785 for the second Earl of Bathurst. Extensive work was done in 1807 by James Wyatt and Thomas Cundy, when the bays and portico were added, turning it into an example of Greek Revival architecture.

Right: *Clandon Park, designed for Lord Onslow some time after 1720, by Giacomo Leoni, the Italian disciple and English publisher of Palladio, who had settled in England. The house is seen here with the addition of a nineteenth-century porch above the original steps.*

FAR-SEEING SIR JOHN SOANE

Many of the designs of John Soane (1753–1837) seem as surprising and innovative today as they did nearly 250 years ago. To walk round his eccentric house (1812–13) at Lincoln's Inn Fields in London, now Sir John Soane's Museum, is an experience of constant surprise. Visual tricks are everywhere, such as its plethora of plane-multiplying mirrors. Coming from a relatively humble background, Soane started his architectural career working for George Dance the younger, moving on to the partnership of Holland and Brown. While studying at the Royal Academy, he won a prize enabling him to go to Rome in 1778 on a travelling scholarship. Returning to London in 1780, he spent several years assiduously building up his practice, and five years later he was earning commissions from all over England.

Sir John Soane, the architect. Advanced beyond this time, he used accepted Neoclassical forms and motifs in an unique and complex way that foreshadowed the architecture of the future.

Soane's public buildings, like his work at the Bank of England, were simple to the point of austerity, but his private commissions, including his own houses, were quite the opposite. A follower of both Inigo Jones, whom he called, 'this great artist, who in his works treated Architecture sometimes as a useful and sometimes as a pleasing Art', and of Vanbrugh, whom he admired for 'his bold flights of irregular fancy', Soane attempted to combine the disciplines of Antiquity with an imaginative spirit. In his seventh lecture to the students of the Royal Academy, in 1815, he defines beauty in architecture thus:

> An edifice can only be considered beautiful when all its parts are in exact Proportion, well balanced and combined together with proper quantities of light and shadow; richness and repose. It must form an entire whole from whatever point it is viewed, like a group of Sculpture . . .

ROYAL PATRONAGE

Royal patronage has always been apparent in architecture. Princes and kings have long commissioned palaces and lodges, dairies and arsenals. Without the undoubted interest of many of these royal patrons in furthering the cause of art—and at the same time furthering their own status—many fine buildings would never have been built. Indeed, the extravagances of Louis XIV, Catherine the Great and Frederick the Great were in large part in the interests of posterity.

FRENCH NEOCLASSICAL DWELLINGS

In France patronage had always shaped the face of architecture. The world of the rich and noble revolved very much around the court and moved with it. Houses were stately and grand, built to reflect might and to entertain in style. Not all private houses were palaces. Gabriel, Soufflot and Ledoux designed houses for the upper classes, whether noble or just plain moneyed. But if they were not palaces, they were still imposing.

French Neoclassical houses flourished in a more urban setting than their English counterparts, based not so much on the designs of Palladio but more on the continuing classical tradition, the legacy of the Sun King, Louis XIV. Soufflot built the Hôtel de Marigny with Palladian proportions for his friend and patron, the Marquis de Marigny, Mme de Pompadour's brother, in 1769. Even the unconventional Ledoux designed conventional Neoclassical houses, like the speedily built Pavillon de Louveciennes for Mme du Barry in 1771 and the Hôtel de Montmorency in Paris.

Horace Walpole described, with more than a touch of irony, the exterior of such a new Gallic house:

> How little and poor all your houses in London will look after this! In the first place you must have a garden half as long as the Mall, and then you must have fourteen windows, each as long as t'other half, looking into it; and each window must consist of only eight frames of looking glass.

Jacques-Ange Gabriel was the earliest Neoclassical architect of them all.

The Pavillon de Louveciennes, built by C.-N. Ledoux for Madame du Barry in 1771. Ledoux designed several buildings for Madame du Barry which were fairly typical of French architecture of the time, before he developed the idiosyncratic and imaginative style of his later work.

He was a follower of Palladio, whose inspiration lay behind Gabriel's design for both the Château de Compiègne and the Petit Trianon. The latter of these, which Gabriel designed for the Marquise de Pompadour and Louis XV, is a fine example of Neoclassicism combined with rococo. The exterior is a rotunda, which seems based on Palladio's designs, while the inside is almost entirely a charming essay in rococo style.

It would be wrong however, to give the impression that all was always *très sérieux* in French architecture. Walpole again, when travelling in France in 1766, remarked:

> On the road to Livry, I passed a new house, on the pilasters of the gate to which were two sphinxes in stone, with their heads coquetly reclined, straw hats and French cloaks slightly pinned and not hiding their bosoms. I don't know whether I or Memphis would have been more diverted.

THE STATELY HOMES OF RUSSIA

In Russia, from the time of Peter the Great, Western architects' ideas and designs were much in demand (see p. 80).

Catherine's palaces, in particular Tsarskoe Selo, and to a lesser degree Pavlovsk, were built in the baroque manner, but altered and added to by an unlikely figure—the Scottish architect Charles Cameron (1740–1812), better known in Russia as Karol Karlovich. Recommended by his friend Clérisseau, Cameron arrived in Russia in about 1779, staying for at least ten years. He worked on the renovations that Catherine wanted at Tsarskoe Selo, the great summer palace of the Tsars, and also built a Cold Bath there, a building now known as the Cameron Gallery, where the influence of Palladio is evident. Later, under Catherine's instructions, he designed the palace at Pavlovsk for her son the Grand Duke Paul and his wife Marie Feodorovna, although he did not get on as well with them as he did with the Tsarina.

Pavlovsk. Cameron's palace here was also commissioned by Catherine, but as a new building it is closer in style than Tsarskoe Selo to buildings being erected at the same time at near-by St Petersburg.

Catherine the Great's palace at Tsarskoe Selo. Redesigned by Charles Cameron at her behest from a baroque original, the building has a flamboyance and sense of drama that marks it out from its contemporaries.

GERMAN ROYALTY AND NEOCLASSICISM

In the independent states of Germany, architecture was an important part of the prestige of each state, several of which wished to imitate the grandeur of Versailles. One of the earliest German Neoclassical architects was Friedrich Wilhelm Freiherr von Erdmannsdorff (1736–1800), who went to the court of Dessau in 1758. He embarked on a long trip to Europe, where he became a friend of Clérisseau and learned to admire the works of Palladio. On his return in 1767, he rebuilt the castle at Dessau for his young patron, Duke Franz von Anhalt. Then came Schloss Wörlitz (1768–73), the first breath of Neoclassicism in Germany.

Friedrich Wilhelm III came to the Prussian throne in 1770. His taste in art and architecture was excellent, and he admired Neoclassicism. The architect Schinkel, who conceived many Neoclassical houses, designed Schloss Glienicke for Prince Karl, one of Friederich's sons, in 1824.

Ludwig I of Bavaria, who reigned from 1825 to 1845, had impeccable, if at times eccentric and self-serving artistic taste. Many of the later Neoclassical houses in and around Munich were built by him, with the help of Klenze, who was Schinkel's opposite number in Bavaria.

Above: *Detail of the Kuppelsaal in the Razumovsky Palais, Vienna, designed in Greek revival style 1806-7 by Louis Montoyer.*

Left: *The Villa Lingg at Bad Schachen, Lindau (on Lake Constance). It was formerly the residence of the poet Hermann Lingg.*

The façade of the Rotonda addition of the Josefbad building at Baden. It was added in 1804 when Neoclassicism was becoming popular in Germany and Austria.

SWEDEN AND THE TESSIN CONNECTION

Sweden had long had architectural and cultural links with France through the father and son architects, the Tessins. Nicodemus Tessin the elder (1615–81), was the royal architect to King Edwidge-Eleonore at Drottningholm for twenty years. After his death his son, Nicodemus the younger (1654–1728), who had spent time in Paris and Rome, became the architect in charge of the reconstruction of the royal palace in Stockholm (from 1697), which had earlier burned down. Both father and son were in constant communication with Paris as to ideas both for architecture and decoration. The Francophile connection was further strengthened when Nicodemus the younger's son, Count Charles-Gustave Tessin (1695–1770), became Swedish Ambassador to France during the reign of Louis XV. The diplomat imported wholesale, French Neoclassical ideas to be incorporated into his house, Åkerö, built to Carl Hårleman's designs in the 1750s.

Under the reign of Gustav III (1771–92), the cultured Swedish king who loved Paris and could speak seven languages, the Antique style was represented by Louis-Adrien Masreliez, who decorated the royal pavilion at Haga. Gustav III spent much of his time recruiting people to work at Haga. All this interest had an effect on other Scandinavians and resulted in a distinctive northern Neoclassicism, an accident of the rococo quite unlike its counterpart farther south. Jean-Louis Desprez produced several schemes for the new residence that the king wanted to build, but none was realized.

Detail of a wall panel at Haga.

Interior of the royal pavilion at Haga. Although Neoclassical in form, and with typical bas relief figures, the swirling veined marble of the columns and their curved octagonal abacuses introduce a distinctively rococo feel.

Monticello, Virginia. Thomas Jefferson's own home, designed by him over a long period of time, incorporated many classical references, both from his study of Ancient architecture and from his interest in Palladio.

AMERICAN NEOCLASSICAL RESIDENCES

In the eighteenth century, American citizens were building houses in their large and virtually empty new country just as fast as they could. American Neoclassical houses are immediately recognizable and could never be mistaken as French, English or German. The classical references are there, but used in a unique way—they are fresh and clean, stamped with a balanced dignity. Often there is the unmistakeable signature of a wooden façade. Thomas Jefferson, the architect–president, built what is still one of the most famous of all Neoclassical villas, Monticello, which he remodelled in 1803, changing his original, rather Palladian design into one that more fully spoke of the new classical.

Throughout the South and along the Eastern seaboard, up into the New England states, houses were built between the years 1780 and 1810 that reflected not the experimental natures of Adam and Soane but, rather, an academic understanding of the Antique. At first the references were Palladian, owing much to the academic example of Burlington and Chambers. As the nineteenth century dawned, however, the influences owed more to the Greek Revival, by now in full swing in Europe. The use of local materials—very often native wood—coupled with façades with columns and porticoes resulted in a homogeneous and harmonious style that was perceptibly American. Books of architectural details were published, containing illustrations of orders and other classical necessities, and ambitious carpenters in every state purchased them, duly adopting and adapting to their tastes (and finances). Until the American Civil War (1861–65) these small temples appeared everywhere, from the Elias Brown house (1836) in Old Mystic, Connecticut, with an immense pedimented portico, to Berry Hill (1835–40) in Virginia, built by its owner, James Cole Bruce, to resemble a little Parthenon.

Custis-Lee Mansion, Arlington, Virginia, remodelled by George Hadfield 1802–17 with a classical portico.

The Greek Revival style in full spate in the Garden District of New Orleans. A purist might find such a grand expression of the style on a house of these proportions somewhat eccentric, but the result is certainly characterful.

Pingree House, Salem, Massachusetts, designed by Samuel McIntire, 1804. A woodcarver by trade, McIntire was a self-taught architect. He was one of the leading practitioners of the Federal style.

Homewood House, Baltimore, Maryland. The Palladian influence was strong on the Eastern seaboard in the late eighteenth century.

GREEK AND ROMAN WALLS AND FLOORS

Interior decoration was very important to both Greeks and Romans. They knew the art of making coloured pigments, and used their knowledge to good effect, painting the walls with designs, or else finishing them with stucco or occasionally marble.

Paintings found in Pompeii show how the early civilizations in Egypt, then Greece and Rome, had learned to combine function and beauty, adding ornament and decoration where necessary. Early Greek houses were relatively simple, though adorned with a degree of colour and decoration. However, by the end of the Roman Empire decoration had become excessive.

Rome, as always, embellished Greek ideas—adding them to indigenous Etruscan forms of decoration until, by Nero's day, virtually every conceivable surface could be covered with decoration, paintings, plasterwork and mosaics. Indeed, by the end of the Roman Empire, some internal walls were awash with paintings—many of them trompe l'oeil, which reached from ceiling to floor.

Floors were regarded as another opportunity for decoration. Often made of mosaic, they were sometimes designed in the form of a carpet, complete with borders and repeating patterns. The art of mosaic design developed extensively before the end of the Roman Empire, evolving from early crude motifs made from washed pebbles to complex pictures of enormous range and beauty made from thousands of small, light-reflecting particles. Although mosaics were naturally used on floors, Pliny the elder wrote of paved floors being laid by the Greeks, as well as marble being used in block form. The Romans also manufactured their own terracotta tiles, setting up kilns in places as far from the hot Mediterranean as cold, hostile Britain.

In fact, decoration was everywhere in classical houses, and an integral part of the Ancients' lives—whether the early simple blocks of colour on walls, as used by the Greeks and the early Romans, or the vastly complicated designs that can be seen in the later works at Pompeii. The colours most often used were black—often employed as a background colour to throw a painting into high relief—red, blue, green and a bright, strong yellow.

Plain walls were rare in Ancient Greece and Rome: they were nearly always decorated, usually divided into panels and either coloured or filled with a design. The art of wall-painting developed in Pompeii, going from the early blocks of plain colour designed to resemble brick or stone to the extremely elaborate painting in the last, Fourth Style, where architectural motifs and cavorting mythological figures were surrounded by ornamental devices. The painted panels were sometimes marked out by trompe l'oeil (literally, 'fool the eye') columns, and such painted follies were widely

The Dionysiac rites on a fresco in the Villa of Mysteries, Pompeii. As with other excavated paintings, the domestic life of the Romans is revealed in clear detail, showing furniture, textiles, and tromp l'oeil *painted decoration in abundance.*

used: several houses even have windows painted on the walls, which show a view of a mythical garden or street life.

Another form of trompe l'oeil was the architectural paintings—wall-paintings showing architectural styles, not in plan form, but as dimensional paintings. Colonnades of columns, peristyles, street fronts and façades, all marched along Pompeiian walls. There were friezes along the tops of walls, designs below the painted dado.

MEDIEVAL HOUSES

But that was a long time ago, in a rich, self-indulgent age. By the twelfth and thirteenth centuries in Northern Europe, few of these finer points of civilized living had much relevance to the life of ordinary people. For most, life was hard and taken day by day. Permanence was no longer a feature of domestic life, and there was little point in spending time and money on the elaborate decoration of walls and floors. In those uncertain times, when most houses were built in a way that made them easily defendable, the criterion was that anything within the house should be portable rather than beautiful, from the bed itself to the floor covers. Luxuries were redefined as objects that could easily be transported and reassembled on arrival at another house. The house itself remained a shell.

The main domestic considerations, for many centuries, were those of practicality: warmth, light and shelter. Rooms, or rather living areas of the house, radiated out from the central hearth, the communal spot where warmth and food could be had. Floors were laid with hard-packed mud or rough-hewn boards, sometimes with rushes on top. Walls were rough-plastered, sometimes with a pattern worked into them, and with simple wooden panelling below.

Furniture, too, was simple, cut from native woods like oak. Woven textiles were in the form of hangings, and used as much for warmth and insulation as decoration.

DWELLINGS IN THE SIXTEENTH AND SEVENTEENTH CENTURIES

Only when a more peaceful period arrived did people start to pay more attention to the permanent fixtures in their homes. During Elizabeth I's reign (1559–1603), for the first time the prospect of constant war seemed less of a certainty, and houses were no longer being built as fortifications. Extravagant nobles, like the eccentric Bess of Hardwick, spent much of their time and money on buildings. Of Hardwick Hall, one of her more grandiose projects, a local rhyme claimed, 'Hardwick Hall, more glass than wall', referring to its massive window-fronted façade.

In sixteenth-century Northern Europe, although a squire's manor house still might not be filled with much permanent luxury, the houses of the nobles were often rich and splendid. Murals were painted, panelling was hung, often in quite elaborate forms, and tapestries were woven. In Italy, of course, the houses, palaces and churches of the Renaissance were almost as fine as those of the Ancients their builders were emulating. And by the late seventeenth century, innumerable houses were finely furnished and hung throughout Europe.

RAPHAEL AND ANCIENT ROME

Things had always been a bit different in Mediterranean countries, however, where traditions handed down from ancestors had never entirely vanished. The art and scope of classical decoration had long been admired in Italy, and were soon brought to the attention of the outside world by Raphael's inspired early sixteenth-century renditions in the Vatican of the *grotteschi* from the underground rooms of Nero's Golden Palace. They were widely noted, but not widely imitated at the time. Although decorative motifs from those paintings and from the five orders, and numerous other devices seen on ruined buildings, were employed, they were rendered without any sense of the culture behind the ornament. But as no full-scale excavations had as yet been done, the full extent of Roman interiors, and what they actually looked like and the motifs they employed, was not known. Until the excavation boom of the 1750s, the only easily seen images were disconnected fragments of walls and ceilings unearthed when buildings were turned over in search of treasures within.

When large-scale excavations started in the early eighteenth century, followed by books with engravings of different monuments and ruins, the inclusion of classical features became a major aspect of interior decoration across Europe. And the more that was excavated, the more that was found. Since decorative ideas were rather easier to export than antiquities, as well as being considerably cheaper, it is not difficult to see why the discoveries were not only greeted with such excitement, but also transferred wholesale into the houses of those returning from the Grand Tour.

LIFE STYLES IN THE GRAND HOUSES

Life at this time in egalitarian England was comparatively relaxed, compared to the rigours of courtly existence in France, although domestic life was far more formal than would be accepted today. At the start of the century, grand houses followed the basic plan of one room succeeding another, and anyone with any pretensions to grandeur boasted the ultimate status symbol, the State Bedroom (originally so called to distinguish it as the bedroom in which a monarch or noble slept), although by the eighteenth century this chamber had generally developed into the best bedroom.

Today it is difficult to comprehend the ritual that was attached to the State Bedroom, but not so difficult when one understands that such a place was considered a reception room, part of a set of formal apartments, and not, as a bedroom is thought of now, a private chamber. Once that concept is understood, it is easier to see the importance of the State Bed. This piece of furniture—dressed with hangings that were often the most expensive thing in the house—represented the way of life that its owner had attained or aspired to attain.

It was inevitable that there would be a reaction against this artificial, almost indigestible formality, and the early Neoclassical movement, particularly in England, was an expression of this. The English monarchy had never enjoyed the same power as the French, and there were now many factors, economic as well as historical, that were turning people towards a new way of domestic life. Always taken by the idea of the power of the individual, as opposed to the state, the demographic and

psychological makeup of the English was changing. Large houses were no longer built or owned only by the enormously rich or the very noble. A new middle class was emerging. Through finance, industry and land, the self-made man of the Age of Enlightenment wanted to live well and comfortably—wishes that did not equate with ideals of excess and formality. Entertainment and public life were still important, but so was the life of the individual, and that of the family. A degree of privacy, and an ability to entertain on a small scale, were required. Thus, the arrangement and position of the various rooms in the new houses that were being built had become an architectural priority.

THE THREE STRAINS OF NEOCLASSICISM

As the Neoclassical movement progressed, design priorities changed, especially in relation to interiors. Broadly, there were three phases, each one appropriate to its time. The earliest of these was Palladianism, with its adherence to the then-new principles of proportion and balance as laid down in the sixteenth-century writings of Andrea Palladio; this in turn was combined with loyalty to the tradition of baroque decoration. The end result was serious, simple exterior architecture with elaborate, rich interiors, full and dark, with much emphasis on gilding, coffered ceilings and grand design.

The second phase of Neoclassicism was epitomized by the work of Robert Adam and his followers, who consciously returned to the actual decoration employed by Ancient Greeks and Romans: light in tone and

shape, using spaces in convex and concave form, and adding everywhere a new delicacy in the final design, coupled with clear colours, cartouches and columns.

And then, finally, there was that Neoclassical strain exemplified by Ledoux and Boullée in France, and Soane in England, wherein the original Neoclassical themes were used in quite a different manner. The design came from massed shapes, dependent less on additional conventional decoration and more on the design itself, using the vocabulary of Ancient architecture but simplified to almost minimalist levels. Light gave the contrasts, and the interest.

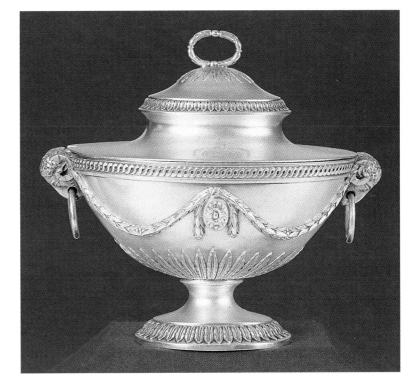

Right: *A sauce tureen by John Carter, who sometimes worked with Robert Adam, in 1744. Completely Neoclassical in form, it follows the shape of ancient urns, bedecked as always with swags, medallions and leaves.*

Right: *An ormolu-mounted clock and calendar, encased in malachite. Made by the firm of Lesieur in Paris in 1819, the pair encapsulates Empire style—the heavy ormolu, swagged and banded, and the ormolu supports fashioned as flaming torchières.*

A pair of lapis oviform vases made in 1760s showing the use of classical detail from medallions to laurel wreaths, with painted decoration, simulating bas relief.

113

THE FIRST PHASE: PALLADIANISM

For the first architectural innovators during the early part of the century, Palladio was the source of inspiration. His books, as well as the houses he built, showed that internal planning was an integral part of architecture. His architectural works showed the arrangement and use of the rooms, as well as the important outer architectural details, and they were far removed from the distant, cold ground plans of French palaces.

Neither Palladio nor anyone else working in the 1500s would have known much about the actual interiors of Ancient homes. Very little thorough excavation had been done at the time Palladio was writing. But, in any case, he did not wish to merely repeat slavishly the perceived rules of the Ancients, or to pretend that his plans followed the shape of rooms in Ancient Rome. Instead, like the good architect he was, he sought and found a contemporary interpretation that was suitable for his patrons, the sixteenth-century landowners of republican Venice.

The Palladians in England, led by the architect-earl, Lord Burlington, studied Palladio's plans closely. From Burlington's design of Chiswick House to Colen Campbell's publication of *Vitruvius Britannicus*, the interior of a house was being taken as seriously as its outside.

Palladio's designs differed from traditional sixteenth-century houses in that instead of a series of rectangular spaces, he had introduced spaces with shapes, and in his hands they could be elliptical, circular, even octagonal. Rooms, too, could be circular, with domed ceilings. Related proportions were everything, private rooms were as important as public and everything was to be simple and in proportion. The hall and saloon were important, and compact service wings kept the main rooms of the house together.

BURLINGTON AND KENT

Burlington and his collaborator William Kent (see pp. 60 and 93) followed Palladio's general precepts, but made some refinements that they felt befitting to a cultured man of the eighteenth century. There was now the sculpture gallery, for example, which in many cases replaced the traditional long gallery. The upper classes had long been interested in 'curiosities', which ranged from cabinets of shells to antiquarian Romano-British remains. The new sculpture galleries were a continuation of that interest. Filled with pieces of Ancient sculpture and broken bits of columns or pediments, they spoke of learning and taste—even if there was some confusion about what the objects actually were. And numerous gentlemen built such galleries, not only those whose houses were large enough to have a long gallery. The Duke of Richmond, the Earl of Burlington and the Earl of Egremont at Petworth, as well as Charles Towneley in Park Street, Westminster, and even Sir William Hamilton in his consul's quarters in Naples, had a place devoted to their antiquarian art, where one could talk with fellow devotees of the delights of the Antique.

Holkham Hall, designed by Burlington, Kent and its owner, the Earl of Leicester, boasted one of the first true Neoclassical interiors in England. The impressive hall, with its complex combination of classical references taken from Palladio's design of a basilica, which he in turn had taken from Vitruvius, was an outstanding success and set the stamp on the new classical style. It was followed by Houghton, the palace built by Colen Campbell for Sir Robert Walpole. Kent was engaged in 1727 to complete the work, and the end result was very elaborate, with much decorated panelling and gilding, furniture especially designed by Kent and one of the finest collections of paintings in Europe.

Decorative styles, both in England and on the Continent, developed at a different pace to styles of architecture, with the early Palladian houses in England far less severe on the inside than they were on the outside. For the first fifty years of the eighteenth century, Neoclassical interiors were still to a great degree hybrid beasts combining the ideals of the English baroque and French classicism. Walls and ceilings were still painted with huge rolling landscapes, clouded skies, ruined cities and other suitable inspirational topics. Painters from Italy, France and sometimes England worked on them. The Italians had been recognized since the Renaissance as the best painters of walls and ceilings in Europe and thus were in great demand in England: the Neapolitan artist Antonio Verrio for example worked in England for much of the last quarter of the 1600s, spending twelve years at Burghley alone decorating ceilings and walls.

WANSTEAD AND WILLIAM KENT

Not all the interior painters were Italian. One of the earliest and most influential English houses in the early eighteenth century, Wanstead, built by Colen Campbell, had on one floor a great hall, two dining rooms, two drawing rooms and a bedchamber, whence a passage led to the ballroom; many of these rooms were grandly painted, including the hall, whose decoration had been undertaken by William Kent and which was described by Walpole, as 'another proof of [Kent's] incapacity'. The ubiquitous Kent, before discovering that his true strengths lay in interior decoration, garden design and architecture, executed a great deal of painting work, promoted in his commissions no doubt by his friend and patron, Lord Burlington. Alas, he really was not very good. Horace Walpole, who actually liked Kent, and thought him a genius in other fields, called him a painter 'below mediocrity'. The writer loathed Kent's portraits, and as for the ceiling paintings he was doing, he further said: 'Kent's drawing was as defective as the colouring of his portraits, and as void of any merit.'

MORE NICHES FOR MORE STATUES

As more Roman temples were unearthed and identified, architects cut curved niches into walls to hold statues and busts, built columns of plaster, stone or marble to emphasize an entrance, and surrounded doors, windows and chimneypieces with pilasters and pediments. By the nineteenth century, as with other aspects of Neoclassicism, it had all got slightly out of hand. Soane had noticed:

> In Modern Works, Statues are variously introduced, generally with as little regard to situation as to character; sometimes on the extremities, or centres of pediments; sometimes in recumbent attitudes on the inclined sides of pediments, and frequently half concealed in niches.

The Great Hall at Kedleston in Derbyshire, designed by Robert Adam, with 8-metre (25 ft) tall columns of Derbyshire alabaster, a floor of grey Hopton marble and, in the coved ceiling, plasterwork by Joseph Rose. Packed with Neoclassical elements, down to the statue-filled niches, it is one of Robert Adam's most dramatic interiors.

A design by Robert Adam for a carpet for the drawing room at Shelburne House, showing how he used Neoclassical designs with the lightest of touches. Adams would often repeat or echo the design of the ceiling in the carpet, making a whole out of disparate parts.

SURFACES AND STAIRCASES

Ceilings were high, domed, coffered and vaulted. Walls were dark and rich in colour, and usually covered with heavy damasks. Gold was used to accentuate details, and to frame paintings. Dados were employed to complement the deep skirtings.

Staircases soared. When not well designed—that is, with a light hand and sure touch— the effect was far from cosy, and many houses felt more like a temple than a home. On the other hand, when all went well, the effect was considerable.

Floors, too, were no longer just rough-cut planks of wood. They were cut to size, although not often polished, and deal or pine was used, as well as oak, and the surfaces could be stencilled or painted. In seventeenth-century France, and in the grander houses in England, marquetry floors became popular, with ever more complex and fine patterns.

The discovery of how to cut marble and stone into manageable, regular patterns, such as the popular black and white squares used in the sixteenth century, meant that patterns that followed the classical could now be designed, incorporating such Antique motifs as the ubiquitous Greek key. Floor tiles were not new, of course, as the Romans had used them.

Although the great carpet factories were Savonnerie and Aubusson in France, English carpets of a high standard were being made. Many eighteenth-century floors were covered with lovely Wilton carpets, and Robert Adam later designed carpets in a Neoclassical vein that were made up by both Axminster and Moorfields.

THE SECOND PHASE: ADAM IN THE FOOTSTEPS OF THE ANCIENTS

The watershed in Neoclassical design—both exterior and interior—came in England with the return, in 1758, of Robert Adam from Rome, and in France around 1756, with the first showing of interest in all things Greek.

Although Adam's quest was the same as that of Lord Burlington some thirty years earlier, the conclusions reached were very different. Whereas Burlington had followed the path of Palladio, Adam wanted to retrace the actual steps, as he saw them, of the Ancients. In other words, he wished to replicate the unadulterated style of the Ancient Greeks and Romans, not as seen through the refining eyes of the sixteenth century, but through the eyes of the originators.

Palladianism had faded as a style in England with the deaths of its chief protagonists: Colen Campbell in 1729, William Kent in 1748 and Lord Burlington in 1753. From now on there was to be no more baroque, for Adam and those he influenced were as far away from the rolling drama of the seventeenth century as it was possible to be. The new style must have been quite staggeringly different to the eyes of a beholder. An Adam room could not have been mistaken for a room designed seventy-five years before. Whereas Celia Fiennes, for example, wrote in 1702 of rooms in Lowther Castle wainscoted in large panels of oak, and with chimneypieces of dark marble, Adam-decorated rooms were full of light and colour—even his most dramatic settings.

KEDLESTON AND SYON HOUSE

Robert Adam approached the design of the rooms themselves in a completely innovative way. He introduced an internal variety in both the arrangement of rooms and their makeup. He did the first of the interiors for which he was to become famous at Kedleston in Derbyshire. In fact he came to the house late, it having been designed first by Matthew Brettingham, and then on his death by James Paine. Kedleston was greatly admired at the time. A contemporary account read: 'The Egyptian Hall is one of the noblest and most magnificent in Europe, and all its ornaments are adapted with so much judgment, and finished in such exquisite taste that the whole forms a scene of genuine edificial grandeur.' However, there was little of the Egyptian in the Hall. Conceived by Paine as a vast columned room, leading from the Corinthian portico, the number of columns was altered from fourteen to sixteen in total by Adam when he took over from Paine in 1761.

Later, at Syon House, home of the Duke of Northumberland, an interested and intelligent patron who had designed his own conservatory, Adam took his ideas even further. Often wrongly perceived in the popular imagination as a mere purveyor of prettiness, Adam could be even more dramatic than his predecessors, as is shown by both the entrance hall at Syon, its contrasting and striking tiled floor incorporating both the Greek key pattern and contrasting diamonds beneath a heavily plastered and domed ceiling, and the anteroom, with Italian marble columns dredged from the Tiber. Indeed, Adam's influence was immense, and so many examples of his work have been preserved that they can almost be seen to comprise a complete study in the art of Neoclassical decoration.

THE EVOLUTION OF ADAM'S STYLE

In 1754, when Adam was in Italy, he had engaged as his companion and tutor the French painter Charles-Louis Clérisseau, who had been in Rome for some time, both at the Académie, and, later, working on his own. Clérisseau's tuition in painting and archaeology taught Adam to see the beauties of classical decoration and, more importantly, how to apply it to contemporary interiors.

In developing his decorative style, Adam took as a basis the disciplines that had gone before, but he then altered them, sometimes in a subtler, sometimes in a more blatant manner. He used colour in a way that was bright, rather than deep, often with less gilding. He commissioned painters and paintings, but chose major artists, like the Royal Academician Angelica Kauffmann, her husband Antonio Zucchi and Giambattista Cipriani; between them, they painted cartouches, roundels, panels and medallions on ceilings, walls, doors and chimneypieces.

The motifs and ornaments that Adam used were an important and easily recognizable element of his style; his genius, however, lay not in the ornaments themselves, but in the way he employed them. Some were taken directly from the classical art and architecture that he knew, like griffins, garlands and swags, scrolls and arabesques; others, like urns, vases, paterae and tripods, were based on Ancient artefacts. He had also seen in Rome the work of the Renaissance architects and painters, like Raphael, and all these later influences were brought together and subsumed into his classically based art.

ADAM'S USE OF STUCCO

Adam used plaster on ceilings, but in a very different manner from the imposing coffered and barrel-vaulted domes of a few years before. Working with him was one of the greatest contemporary stucco workers, Joseph Rose, who understood Adam's vision of plaster as a near-plastic material to be used, almost like fabric, draped and turned into amazingly fluid designs. In the hands of Rose, stucco became malleable, almost forming itself into ovals and circles, and strong central motifs that often echoed or complemented the carpet below. Walls were also embellished with Rose's plaster masterpieces. At Syon House for example, in the majestic Ante Room, Rose modelled huge gilded bas relief trophies, to stand between the Antique columns.

There was actually a difference between plaster, strengthened with animal hair, and stucco, mixed with marble dust. Stucco was the newer development and those like the Rose family moulded it into the lightest and most ribbonlike of designs. Robert Adam always used a special mixture called Liardet's preparation, which had been patented by John Liardet and which the Adams had the sole rights to use. The hot plaster mixture was pressed into moulds, producing a finely detailed positive; its composition meant that it could be applied while still malleable.

After Adam came a succession of good Neoclassical architects working in a simpler yet similar vein. There was Henry Holland, who used Neoclassical design in a simple, classical manner, and James Wyatt, who showed how the early Neoclassical style had matured and deepened—particularly so in the Etruscan Room and Library at Heveningham.

The Red Drawing Room at Syon House, designed by Robert Adam with walls lined in crimson silk woven in Spitalfields. The imposing ceiling, with decorations by Angelica Kauffmann, is based on Raphael's decorated ceiling at the Villa Madama.

The vaulted library ceiling at Kenwood House in Highgate, designed by Robert Adam for the Earl of Mansfield in 1767. Any remaining flat surfaces are decorated with paintings and plasterwork in curves and circles. Adam used conventional Neoclassical elements in a new, fresh way, even down to the clear colours that were inimitably his own.

A panel in the Pompeiian Music Room at Stowe—painted at the height of the Athenian vogue by Vincenzo Valdre between 1777 and 1780.

A RICH REPERTOIRE OF MOTIFS

From Adam in England to Percier and Fontaine in France, the instantly recognizable thing about Neoclassical design was the decorative motifs that characterized it. Based on designs found in Greek and Roman ruins, these devices were used on everything from china to wallpaper.

The decorations originally employed by the Egyptians, Greeks and Romans were largely inspired by the products of nature found all around them in the fields and woods. The rosette, used first by the Egyptians, is thought to come from the lotus flower, and corn, papyrus and the palmette are Egyptian, the latter based on the lotus leaf. The Greeks and Romans transformed the honeysuckle into the anthemion, and used a stylized form of the laurel and myrtle wreaths presented to victors. The scroll, or volute, and the furled leaves of the acanthus were used to decorate columns. Animals and birds appeared on furniture, their heads on chair fronts, their feet or claws as legs. There were more worldly motifs, too, like medallions and trophies. In Antique art a trophy commemorated a battle victory, as did a sculptured group of weapons, helmets and breastplates, often copies of the victor's armour.

This rich design repertoire was used—first by the Ancients, then by their imitators—in many elaborate variations. Laurel and other leaves were shown in trailing swags or festoons; acanthus foliage was used in plaster bands around cornices, or carved in wood around doors. Military trophies were still used as tributes in the eighteenth century, though not often to battles; instead they were often applied to the arts—music, painting, literature, and even to gardening, with fanciful compositions featuring rakes, spades and hats.

Classical motifs were used in more ingenious ways, too. On stairways, the balusters and newels could be carved in classical shapes, such as wreaths or elongated urns. Likewise, around doors, in the middle of panels and on the ceiling—where, particularly in Robert Adam's hands, the whole art of Neoclassical interior decoration reached an apotheosis—such devices abounded, and in the handsomest guises. The ceiling was, above all (in more ways than one), the Neoclassical architect's canvas. From Kent to Soane, by way of Robert Adam, it became in the eighteenth century the signature and the starting point for the design of the whole room.

Far right: *The Pompeiian Gallery at Packington Hall, designed around 1785 by the Fourth Earl of Aylesford and Joseph Bonomi, who had been a pupil of Clérisseau. The strong colours, ornamental motifs and paintings themselves are direct representations of archaeological discoveries.*

Right: *A design for the newly restored Painted Room at Spencer House. Conceived by James 'Athenian' Stuart, and executed from 1759, the room caused a stir when first seen.*

The library at Sledmere in Yorkshire, a house reconstructed in replica after a fire in 1910. Originally designed by the famous plasterer Joseph Rose with Sir Christopher Sykes, the ceiling of the library is vaulted in ancient Roman style, but decorated in a manner that is wholly Neoclassical.

ORNAMENTED CEILINGS

In the classical world the ceiling had always provided an opportunity to create a work of originality and beauty. Faced with a large expanse of virgin plaster, what artist could resist decorating it with stucco or paint? From the earliest times, ceilings were ornamented—sometimes with paintings, sometimes in a multidimensional manner using plaster or stucco to create the design. Roman villas boasted ceilings that were an art form in themselves. Several houses excavated in Pompeii had coffered ceilings with boxed panels. From medieval castles to Renaissance palaces, princes and popes alike demanded that their ceilings be grand and beautiful, and they were duly executed by the greatest painters of the time, from Raphael to Michelangelo. By the seventeenth century, ceilings had come to be all-important in England and France as well. Plaster or stucco work in intricate geometric patterns was an integral part of their decoration, and Inigo Jones, François Mansart and other baroque architects made them appear dazzlingly three-dimensional.

Because of the importance of these painted and stuccoed ceilings, the very best artists were employed to paint them. It is remarkable how, although communications were so comparatively difficult, a small army of French and Italian painters—not to mention stucco workers, carvers and gilders—travelled around Europe from the 1600s, accomplishing the superior decoration for which they were famous. And there were fine artists as well as craftsmen decorating ceilings, among them Angelica Kauffmann, who lived mostly in Rome, where she worked as a portrait painter, and Domenico Bardoli, also originally a portrait painter in Rome. From Scotland to St Petersburg, these talented artists and craftsmen went back and forth, so that not only art, but also considerable information and inspiration, was transmitted in this way.

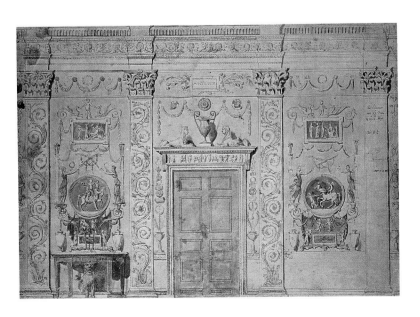

THE STRONG TONES OF NEOCLASSICISM

The walls of a Neoclassical interior were intended to emulate wall-paintings in Ancient Rome, in both strength and tone, and the colours used in Roman interiors became stronger as the centuries passed. Designs done by early Neoclassical architects were strong as well. There is no reason to believe that designers such as Adam would have lowered the strength of tone when creating the designs based on the Antique. Often today, so-called Georgian colours are re-created in sophisticated, subtle shades. In fact, the usual reason that original eighteenth-century colours now appear subtle is because they have faded. Georgian colours were bright—some might even say lurid—and the colours of the Empire in France were even brighter and stronger. Greens could be acid, yellows lemon, purples virulent.

THE ARCHITECT AS EXTERIOR AND INTERIOR DECORATOR

The architect in the eighteenth century was responsible for the house as a whole, both inside and out. Interior decorators and designers were a phenomenon of the future—the first decorator was probably Edith Wharton, the American writer, in the late nineteenth century. Earlier, in the seventeenth century and into the beginning of the eighteenth, the most important figure in the design of the house was the upholsterer. It was he who was responsible for the fabrics that went to cover chairs, windows and, most importantly, beds—the hangings of which were still a major item of expenditure in most grand houses. Later, in the nineteenth century, the upholsterer again rose to prominence: the layers of befringed and tasselled fabrics that ran riot around windows, and across chairs, sofas, tables, beds and even pianos, owed much to his suggestions.

But at the beginning of the eighteenth century, this state of affairs had not yet come to pass. And that is probably the reason why the spaces and the rooms of early eighteenth-century houses seem such an integral part of the whole, all working together, each part arrived at with such care. Today, when any number of different decorating styles can be imposed onto an architectural shell, the result can be a cacophonous confusion. Then, from chair to chimneypiece, and taking in carpets and floor, all was one. Unfettered by excessive frills and furbelows, the greater simplicity of the architect's art would shine through. The new Neoclassical architects understood this. From Burlington and William Kent through Chambers, Adam and Soane, responsibility was taken for all.

WINDOWS GROW IN IMPORTANCE

Windows were highly important in Neoclassical design. Light was vital, and curved Venetian windows were an interesting alternative on a façade.

These were so called because of their use by Palladio and his followers in conjunction with two more conventional windows. Top lighting—often circular—was used by both Soane and Dance to give depth to their internal designs, arches and half-domed ceilings.

THE CHIMNEYPIECE AS CENTREPIECE

The chimneypiece had for some time been considered by many architects the most important piece of design in the house. Advances in the mining industry meant that coal was more easily available, and with servants to carry it, the huge log-burning hearths of the past were no longer essential. But although they had diminished somewhat in size, fireplaces were no less imposing, and still dominated and set the tone for the room. Like a painting, the chimneypiece became the perfect vehicle to exhibit the architect's knowledge, both of classical design and contemporary techniques and materials. Early in the century, chimneypieces were called one or two storey, depending on how far they went up the wall. They might have architraves or pilasters held up by hefty caryatids, and be made from marble or alabaster. On the chimney breast itself was a central ornament, sometimes a looking-glass, combined with gilding or stucco work, sometimes a painting and sometimes relief work in stucco alone. Another sign of the times was the fine fire irons, often designed in the Neoclassical vein, which were emerging from the new industrialized ironworks.

Their dominant position in a room—truly the focal point—meant that chimneypieces represented the design philosophy of their creators. Those of Adam were lighter in tone, with Neoclassical motifs in relief; by contrast, fifty years later the chimneypieces designed by Egypt- and Greece-loving Thomas Hope were framed with griffins, sphinxes and other symbolic motifs.

A marble fireplace at Syon House, designed by Robert Adam, and executed by Domenico Bartoli in the 1760s. Made in marble and scagliola, the design was much more restrained than fireplaces of fifty years before, with Neoclassical motifs in relief, the whole framed with Ionic columns.

Right: *The fireplace in the Etruscan Room, the dressing room at Osterley Park, designed by Robert Adam, and painted between 1775-9. Done nearly twenty years after Athenian Stuart's room at Spencer House, the colours are subtler, the whole more measured, and the fireplace is filled with a painted chimneyboard.*

STAIRCASES SET THE STAGE

Because of the rearrangement of public and private rooms within an interior, and because there were often more and smaller public rooms, which could now be on either the ground or first floor, the staircase was suddenly very important, setting the tone as it did for the splendours to come. Although the design of the staircase had exercised the minds of architects before the eighteenth century—many an early crude house had been lifted by its carved and turned central staircase—it was not until now that this once-utilitarian piece of essential equipment developed into a masterpiece of imagination and design, with drawings being published by everyone from William Chambers to Batty Langley. In any house of importance the central staircase was the primary element. John Soane called them 'the very touchstones of sound knowledge and real merit in the architect'. New houses literally revolved around them, particularly since, following Palladio, the staircase was often double, swinging away from either side of the ground floor to meet again on the first.

Staircase design was also affected, indirectly, by the new developments taking place in the iron industry. The great cast-iron bridge, a monument to progress, was erected at Coalbrookdale in 1779. Ironworks were now built that could use coke in the furnaces. These new furnaces were run at higher temperatures, which meant that the iron being worked became softer and more malleable. Balusters, rails and many other soon-to-be-essential parts of interior design could now be made using this new cast iron, which was also cheaper, if of a lesser quality, than the old wrought iron. This material was widely used on the new staircases, and in Paris it became the fashion to combine cast iron and cast brass—the former for the scrolls and rails, the latter for the more delicate work. Gabriel's railings for the Château de Compiègne were a fine example of this new vogue.

THE RISE OF THE COLUMN

Fashion played as large a part in the design of interiors in the eighteenth century as it does today. Take the inexorable rise, both metaphorically and physically, of the column. Classical architecture was circumscribed by the column. In early buildings, it was used at first as a practical outer supporting device, which was derived, thought architectural theorist Abbé Laugier, from primitive Greek buildings using tree trunks as supports. It developed into an important part of temple and monument design, and became the immediately recognizable symbol of Ancient classical design.

The decoration and shape of the column were originally defined by the Roman architect Vitruvius, who termed the types of column the 'Five Orders'. An order was a column with a base, shaft, capital and entablature, and it should be ornamented and proportioned in one of the five prescribed manners: Doric, Tuscan, Ionic, Corinthian or Composite.

The earliest Doric order was, as used by early Greek builders, a simple, unadorned column narrowing at the top, with no base and no ornamentation; it was named after its inventors, the Dorian Greeks. The Tuscan was as simple as the Doric, and the Ionic, named for the Ionian Greeks, had more ornamentation than both, with a deep shaft from which the column rose up to end in a volute or scrolled capital. The Corinthian was ornamented with furled acanthus leaves, and the Composite was a late

The Print Room at Blickling Hall, Norfolk. In this English style of interior decor, engravings of classical views, framed with borders or friezes of antique motifs, were applied directly to the wall. The decorative effect is far from frivolous, with more than a hint of the moral benefit to be gained by the contemplation of the monuments of the past.

A detail of the Kenwood library ceiling designed by Robert Adam in 1767 (see p. 120). Fluted and gilded composite capitals support a ceiling of ornate gilded plasterwork, using much of the classical repetoire of motifs: lions, trailing wreaths, rams' heads, medallions and urns all play their part.

Roman amalgamation of elements of both the Ionic and Corinthian orders, combining as it did furled acanthus leaves and scrolled volutes. Without exception, these orders were used throughout the known Ancient world, wherever the Greeks and Romans stayed long enough to put up even the smallest shrine.

The definitions of the orders were repeated by Palladio and by every architectural writer after him, including William Chambers and Piranesi, the latter of whom went into the matter in some depth, publishing *Della Magnificenza ed architettura dei Romani* in 1761, with detailed drawings of both Greek and Roman orders.

Columns were first introduced in Britain during the seventeenth century, used as ornamental surrounds for front doors and for the general adornment of the façade. By the beginning of the eighteenth century, columns were used outside, inside, everywhere. The straight rectangular lines and solid masses of Neoclassical architecture gave columns an importance it is difficult to exaggerate, and they were used to outline a door space, to surround a chimneypiece and, importantly, to register intervals within a large room or hall.

THE OVERUSE AND ABUSE OF THE COLUMN

Taken up by all Neoclassical architects and designers, from the Palladians on, as the symbol of all that was good and great about Ancient architecture, the column developed, in some cases by the end of the Neoclassical period and into the 1800s, into just another decorative device, used far too often, and sometimes in the most inappropriate places.

'Mean, paltry and disgusting, and sometimes even ridiculous,' spluttered John Soane, when lecturing to students of the Royal Academy in 1809 on the by then almost universal habit of using the column as a decorative device inside a house, instead of just on the exterior. 'It is doubtful' he went on, 'whether the Greeks and Romans used columns in the interior of their houses, there is no example to be found at Pompeii, nor in the remains of the Villa of Adrian [sic], nor does Pliny speak of them when describing his Villa.' Indeed, within the excavations of Pompeii and Herculaneum, columns were only to be seen outside houses. They lined the atrium and supported colonnades, pergolas and peristyles, but as interior decoration they played a small part—except as painted representations.

Although many early architects, including Soane himself, had used columns—and used them successfully—as internal structures and decoration, he obviously felt that by the time of his Royal Academy lecture it had all gone too far; he then went on to explain that the column is a thing of scale and ought always to convey an idea of magnitude, superiority and marked distinction. Not only did Soane think it was incorrect to use columns inside, but he further believed that columns were not a device that worked in the smaller domestic settings in which they all to often appeared:

> Private houses are in general not sufficiently large for the admission of columns. If of small dimensions, as in the alcoves of bedrooms, all the parts being brought near the eye, the whole appears heavy and misplaced.

PAINTING TO A PLAN

John Cornforth and John Fowler, in their book, *English Decoration in the Eighteenth Century*, explained that when these classical rooms were first designed—with or without pilasters—they were painted in a particular way, in order to create a properly balanced room, with each element of architecture given equal balance. The plan of painting is based on the orders of the column, whether or not there are any columns in the room. They continued: 'The wall surface, whether it is wood panelled or plaster, corresponds to the base, shaft and capital of the column. The dado and skirting correspond to the pedestal, and the entablature corresponds to that of the full order.'

Cornforth and Fowler also pointed out that particular tones of colour should be used for the different sections:

> The flat of the skirting should be the darkest tone, and if not marbled, be painted a blue-berry black rather than a dead black. In a neo-classical room the skirting was sometimes painted in a darker shade of the colour used for the main walls. The skirting mouldings and the dado mouldings should correspond with the cornice and architrave of the entablature. If the entablature is enriched, the mouldings of the skirting and the dado are also enriched; and so if the former is picked out in gold or with colour, the latter should be too. The dado itself is usually white, but if it is painted a colour . . . a shade darker than that of the main fields of the walls is used instead. Provided that the colours used, or the tones of the same colour if there is only one, are properly balanced, the relationship of horizontals and verticals will be correct.

NEOCLASSICISM IN FRANCE

France, the acknowledged leader in all matters of style and decoration, developed the Neoclassical style a little later than England, and in a different form. Although so near geographically, politically and economically they were far apart.

By the end of the seventeenth century, France was the most powerful country in Europe, and indeed the world. It was important to the French that this supremacy be reflected not only in the many palaces of the king, but also in the homes of all who could afford to build and embellish them.

Louis XIV was the master builder: he started when he came to the throne in 1643 and continued throughout his reign, always in the grand classical manner. Not only was there the new palace of Versailles, which took forty-two years to complete, but the châteaux of Fontainebleau, St Germain and Compiègne were also improved and enlarged. The magnificence of his schemes was unparalleled, and all promoted the power and greatness of the king.

The whole court was expected to remain in constant attendance on the king at Versailles, which was considered the centre of everything. Its wonders—its many amazing rooms, decorations and paintings, the likes of which had never been seen before—were spoken of with awe all around the civilized world. The layout, or planning, of the rooms was formal beyond anything built before or since, but it was suitable for the royal family, who lived their daily lives, from their dressing at the *grande levée* to their undressing at the *grande couchée*, in public. The palace's chambers, some of which were given the names of planets, were designed as a progression of vast formal reception rooms, decorated and gilded in a fashion that made even the most jaundiced or jaded of observers stand up and stare.

Architecturally, Louis XIV's influence throughout the rest of Europe was extremely extensive. France was recognized from the end of the seventeenth century to be the leader in style. The standards were set there, and others merely imitated. Encouraged, or possibly goaded, into action, there were those in England and other European countries who began to produce mansions and palaces that, while not aspiring to quite such Gallic grandeur, at least paid more than lip service to the concept of a beautiful interior.

THE REIGN OF LOUIS XV

Although there was progressively less ritual under both Louis XV and Louis XVI and Marie Antoinette, life at the French court was still just as detached from reality. During Louis XV's reign, the public *levées* and *couchées* continued for the whole family at Versailles; there are numerous contemporary accounts of the way the whole court literally ran from room to room to be in the right place when the king entered, or when the queen was dining.

The ever-observant Horace Walpole described his presentation at a *levée* at Versailles in 1765:

> You are let into the king's bedchamber just as he has put on his shirt; he dresses and talks good-humouredly to a few, glares at strangers, goes to mass, and a-hunting. The good old queen . . . is at her dressing table attended by two or three old ladies . . . . Thence you go to the dauphin, for all is done in an hour. He scarce stays a minute . . . . The dauphiness is in her bedchamber, but dressed and standing; looks cross, is not civil, and has the true Westphalian grace and accents. The four mesdames . . . stand in a bedchamber in a row . . . looking good humoured, not knowing what to say. Then you are carried to the dauphin's three boys who you may be sure only bow and stare . . . the whole concludes with seeing the dauphin's little girl dine, who is round and as fat as a pudding.

HOUSES OF THE WEALTHY PARISIANS

French social life still revolved around the court to a certain degree, but, as in England, there was by the middle of the eighteenth century a new class of prosperous men—mainly financiers and industrialists—and they were building houses within Paris itself, which was expanding rapidly. Much trouble was taken and much money spent by these new rich to establish themselves as leaders in comfort, style and taste. Houses were richly decorated and very elaborate, and the watchful Horace Walpole wrote of a

OTHER FRENCH HOUSES

In the days before he explored the revolutionary, Claude-Nicholas Ledoux built and decorated the Hôtel de Montmorency with many classical allusions. For Mme du Barry's Pavillon de Louveciennes, he included a peristyle, Ionic columns and classical ornamental motifs.

Charles de Wailly, too, in his remodelling work on the Hôtel d'Argenson for the Marquis de Voyer, installed vaulted ceilings and caryatids in the dining room, and in the salon arched doors and windows separated by relief wreaths. This last was worked on in the 1760s, by which time the news of the excavations at Herculaneum and Pompeii was reaching Paris and London.

NEOCLASSICISM IN RUSSIA

Between Percier and Fontaine's Empire style in France, England's Regency period (named after the Prince Regent, the future George IV) and, earlier, the richness of design admired by that lover of Western taste, Catherine the Great of Russia, there was a stylistic connection. Some of the similarities perhaps can be explained by the coincidental arrival on the world scene of heads of state who, each in his or her own way, wished to impose a new, personal style, either politically, as with Napoleon and Catherine the Great, or socially, as with the Prince Regent. Another more obvious reason was that, as in the early days of the century, there was still an international nexus between architects, artists and designers, who exchanged views and ideas and often travelled between the different capitals of the world.

In Russia, for example, where Neoclassical architecture took longer to become established than in Britain, the Scottish architect Charles Cameron had been engaged by Catherine the Great in 1779. Tsarskoe Selo, which had been built thirty years earlier by Rastrelli for the Tsarina Elizabeth, was in need of renovation. In addition to that, Catherine, a self-confessed Anglophile—certainly as far as houses and gardens were concerned—wanted Cameron to add some apartments to the palace. As was usual then, he was as concerned with the building's interior as its exterior, particularly in the details of his own Cameron Gallery. For these rooms, he designed and commissioned all the components, from the silk hangings to the folding armchairs to the *torchères*. It made for a highly unified finished effect.

Catherine was always ready to spend money on the best. In the First Apartment of the palace, which Cameron designed the year he arrived in Russia, he used gold leaf, marble, crystal, fabric and marquetry, combining them in a rich and sumptuous mixture. Ornament, decoration and gilding abounded, even on the skirting. The finished look was neither baroque nor rococo. Its basis was Neoclassicism, but there was a richness that set it apart from the pedantic rooms of the Empire, or the relatively well-bred restraint of the English Regency. The intensity and warmth of Russian life are captured in those interiors, all the more surprisingly, since they were executed by a foreigner. Despite the little time he had in which to attune to Russian tastes, Cameron succeeded in mixing the exoticism of the East with the style of the West, and the whole effect was far nearer the living quarters of the later Roman emperors than anything William Kent or Robert Adam had ever conceived.

A chased gilt tray made by Anton Ratkov in Moscow, in 1780, during the reign of Catherine the Great. By this time fine workmanship and classical themes were no longer the exclusive province of the West, but were made too in the East, albeit with an inimitably Russian stamp.

NEOCLASSICISM LOSES TOUCH WITH THE CLASSICAL

After Jean-Charles Delafosse published the *Nouvelle iconologie historique* in 1768, which provided a body of Greek-influenced, and often very imaginative, classical ornament, *le goût grec* swept France, with apparently Greek motifs decorating everything from furniture to hairstyles. Like chinoiserie, it was a light, short-lived fashion, but it was also the forerunner of the more serious Greek Revival movement that made itself felt some years later.

Throughout the Neoclassical period, however, even taking into account the amount of informed research that went on in order to ensure accurate replication in the manner of the Ancients, and even in some of Robert Adam's inspired designs, there is a sense of distance from the vitality of the original. Perhaps the relative formality of life in the eighteenth century, and the insistence on good taste at all times, had taken its dampening toll. The concern with correct proportions and properly graded columnar divisions seemed to detract from the life of the real thing. Those whimsical touches that Pompeiian artists seemed to enjoy so much—the small trompe l'oeil windows in the House of the Cryptoporticus, each painted to open onto a different scene; the mosaic of a dog, tied to a half-open door and blocking the way; the painting of a cherub frightened by a flapping duck—are not to be seen in eighteenth-century renditions. By the time so many centuries later that the classical became the Neoclassical, it seemed to have lost much of its immediacy, becoming endowed instead with a specious, conventional and often uninspirational aura of respect.

As the century grew and aged, so did Neoclassical decoration which became richer, heavier, more solid. There were signs of the impending revolutions—political and industrial—in the ever more ornate trappings of design.

THE EARLY GREEK MOVEMENT IN BRITAIN

In Britain, the beginnings of the Greek movement had been heralded much earlier than in France, by James 'Athenian' Stuart. On his return from Athens, after which he was acknowledged as the Greek specialist, he had designed a small Greek temple for the grounds of Hagley Hall in 1758, based not on one particular building, but containing elements taken from several different Greek sources. This caused an enormous amount of interest, and before long Greek temples and shrines were springing up in gardens and parks all over England and the rest of Europe.

At around the same time, in 1759, Stuart designed the now restored Painted Room at Spencer House in London, which was based on Antique motifs, called 'grotesques' (see p. 14). The designs, which sometimes incorporated figures, objects, garlands and wreaths, were framed by oval or rectangular panels and were always used in a formal, geometric fashion. There had been rooms with this sort of overall decoration, loosely based on the *grotteschi*, since artists first went to Rome. One of the first, the Painted Parlour at Rousham, had been designed by William Kent around 1740. But Stuart's was different. Instead of using the motifs in a completely decorative way, he attempted, like Robert Adam, to exactly imitate the designs of Antiquity. Later, other rooms were done based on such motifs.

In 1777 Vincenzo Valdre painted 'Pompeiian Panels' in the Music Room at Stowe, and Joseph Bonomi decorated the extraordinary Pompeiian Gallery at Packington Hall in Warwickshire for Lord Aylesford around 1782 on the same theme. Adam himself designed an Etruscan Dressing Room, in 1775 at Osterley, as did James Wyatt at Heveningham.

PURE GREEK REVIVAL

Some years later, this initial interest in Greek design came to flower as the Greek Revival of the nineteenth century. Excavations and archaeological work continued as they had in the eighteenth century, but the bias was more on scholarship, less on treasure hunting. Public interest was intense, and everywhere public buildings and houses in Britain were being designed, in effect, to resemble transplanted Athenian temples. Inside these edifices, however, the Greek influence showed itself in less ponderous ways, such as plainer surfaces and less decoration.

George Dance the younger was as Greek in terms of interiors as he was in his exteriors. Considered avant-garde, his designs for the interior of Stratton Park, a Greek Revival mansion that he built around 1806, had the simplicity of a temple, combined with the colours of Pompeii.

ENGLAND'S THIRD STRAIN OF NEOCLASSICISM: SOANE

George Dance's pupil, John Soane (see pp. 66 and 100) designed many interiors for others, but arguably his art can be seen in its best light in his own house in Lincoln's Inn Fields, London. Speaking on architecture, he said:

> Every part must be distinct. Rectangular Rooms should communicate with Circular Rooms, and those in turn with Rectangular, and again with others of Mixed Form, the whole in regular gradation both as to quantity as well as shape. Always remembering that it is in the judicious combination of different figures that the mind of a great Architect shows itself.

And in Lincoln's Inn Fields he put theory into practice. There, nothing is as it seems: a ceiling is surrounded by another ceiling; top lighting through circular windows acts as a dramatic spotlight; convex mirrors displace the scene. Ornament is light, based on Greek motifs, and surfaces are bare.

Opposite: *The Breakfast Room in John Soane's London house, designed by himself. Colours are dark and rich, and top lighting, staggered ceilings, and angled mirrors are all easily recognizable Soane signatures.*

In the dining room of John Soane's house, a classical bust set high on the wall is faced by a convex mirror—a Soanian touch—set unusually high on the wall.

THE POPULAR PUBLISHED DESIGNS OF THOMAS HOPE

Thomas Hope (1769–1831), on the other hand, saw ornament as an essential part of decoration. A man of the Regency era, he was born in Holland and later travelled widely for eight years in Egypt as well as Europe. In 1799 he bought a house in London that Robert Adam had designed, redecorating it in his own personal style. He designed everything from the furniture to the arrangement of the rooms in the Duchess Street dwelling, in part to instruct others on the virtues of classical taste, and in particular the Greek Revival.

Not only Greek, but also Roman and Egyptian, decoration could be seen in Hope's house, and in 1807 he published *Household Furniture and Interior Decoration from Designs by Thomas Hope*, which showed the Duchess Street schemes, as well as many examples of classical ornament. The book was mainly a collection of drawings, with full descriptions of the pieces' and rooms' merits, including what he called 'embellishments' like 'trophies, caryatids, griffins, chimaeras, scenic masks, sacrificial implements'. Being a rich amateur, with enough money to publish and publicize his own designs, probably made Hope more influential than another of the same talent but less means might have been, but there is no denying *Household Furniture* was widely read and acted upon.

That same year, 1807, Hope bought a house in Surrey, Deepdene, which he made into a temple for Greek and Egyptian decoration. It was described by J.C. Loudon, somewhat pompously, not to say sycophantically, as '... a group [of buildings] so rich in classic forms and combinations, that no one can duly appreciate its beauties, whose mind is not thoroughly imbued with Italy and the fine arts. It is in short, an example of what the Germans would call the ecstatic in architecture.'

THE FIRST INTERIORS MAGAZINE

The printing and distribution of books and magazines became easier in the early nineteenth century. At around the same time that Thomas Hope was proselytizing, Rudolf Ackermann published a magazine, *Repository of the Fine Arts*, in monthly parts from 1809 until 1828, making the new designs available to a wide audience. A disciple of Thomas Hope, Ackermann published furniture designs from, among others, George Bullock and George Smith. Schemes for curtains and draperies were regularly shown in the magazine, with the additional exciting innovation of tiny scraps of real fabric pasted to the pages. The *Repository* was not merely a catalogue of designs, but was more like a specialist interiors magazine of today.

FRONT OF THE HOUSE

SCALE

Two sofas designed by Robert Adam in the 1770s. Neoclassical architects often designed not just the interiors but furniture and ornaments to go in them.

Left: *Thomas Hope's Deepdene, the front, drawn by John Britton. Hope filled his house with antiquities and with his own Greek Revival Furniture.*

THE FRENCH REVOLUTION AND
THE EMPIRE STYLE

The Revolution the rise of Napoleon altered the development of Neoclassicism.

In 1791, Charles Percier and his friend and partner Pierre-François-Léonard Fontaine formed an interior decorating partnership in Paris. Previously, Percier and Fontaine had studied together in Paris, under the influential architect Peyre, and then had both gone to Rome for several years. In 1798 they were asked to decorate the house of the banker Récamier and his beautiful wife Juliette. The Hôtel Récamier caused a sensation. It was very expensively done, full of gilded wood, dark in colour with bronze and ormolu decoration, and with many Greek and Egyptian references. In 1801 Percier and Fontaine began to publish, in installments, their *Recueil de décorations intérieures*, which explained their classical views and showed many examples of their architectural and decorative ideas. From chimneypieces to bronze mounts, all elements of interior decoration were described and depicted in careful detail.

In 1799, after a coup d'état, Napoleon became first consul of the French Republic. Five years later he was Emperor. Like the kings he had replaced, Napoleon understood the necessity of building around himself outward manifestations of his power. For that, as always in France, architecture and decoration were the answers, and it was to Percier and Fontaine that he turned in 1802. The Empire style had been conceived.

The new middle classes, anxious to own something novel that was not associated with the Ancien Regime, and keen to be seen emulating the Emperor, took up *le style Empire* in a big way. In no time, Napoleon's taste was copied with ease, for he commissioned so much work that Percier and Fontaine soon had a team of architects and artisans working on his different projects, both public and domestic, hence providing a multitude of examples for the Emperor's subjects to follow.

In no other style of decoration, and at no other time, have the motifs of a style been so important, nor so repeated, almost ad nauseam. The wealth of this new society was reflected by the decoration involved in any design. The amount of ornament employed in any house was directly related to the amount of money available. Decorating was not cheap, and could indeed lead to bankruptcy. As well as the more familiar Greek and Roman symbols, Egyptian motifs figured largely during the Empire as a reminder of Napoleon's campaigns there. Military references abounded—trophies, helmets, spears, used singly or combined.

Gone were the semicircular flowing rooms of Adam's time. Empire furniture, with its straight, definite lines, was better seen in rectangular rooms. It was placed along a rectangular axis, with chairs lined neatly against the walls. The new ruling classes, while displacing the old formality, replaced it with another. The colours were strong: dark crimson, royal blue, rich green, gold and purple.

The variety of ways that fabric was put to use in France during the Empire was infinite. Beds had fabric that hung from central coronets or was draped over a canopy. Draped fabric was caught over day beds or panelled in folds against a wall. Campaign memorabilia in the guise of spear-headed poles sat above windows and supported clouds of muslin or gauze. New designs, all in the Empire style, flooded from the factories. These fine fabrics, needed in such quantities, were not cheap, and orders for them, coupled with work that Napoleon commissioned for his houses and palaces, both old and new, gave a new lease on life to the silk factories of Lyons.

The beautiful Madame Récamier, as painted by François-Pascal-Simon Gerard, personified French Neoclassical style, dressed à la Greque, *and seated on a Greek-inspired chair against a suitably classical background.*

A white silk wall hanging of around 1800, embroidered with multicoloured chenille threads. Although the design is an informal interpretation of Neoclassical motifs, there remain traditional elements, such as the Pompeiian border.

THE GROWING IMPORTANCE OF TEXTILES

Textiles had been used in the home for many centuries, first as insulation and for warmth and, later, with the invention of windows, with decorative as well as practical intent. As glass and windows became larger, and a move was made through much of Europe to introduce a reception room—the *piano nobile*—onto the first floor, so curtains and blinds became all-important. Although in England the French Huguenot immigrants working at Spitalfields produced some fine fabrics, the French and the Italians were still pre-eminent in the field: the Italians with heavy cut velvets made around Genoa, the French with silk looms in Lyons, woven tapestries and printed cottons at Jouy.

Lyons had long been very important in the production of fine textiles, not only in France but throughout Europe. Louis XIV had established the silk industry at Lyons, and during the reigns of the three Louis the industry expanded. Designs changed swiftly with different fashions, and eighteenth-century French history may be read through the pattern-books of Lyons. The Revolution, however, dealt a blow to the silk weavers, and Napoleon had to revive the industry. The uniformity of the Empire style meant that designers at Lyons—men like Philippe de Lasalle and Jean-François Bony—could work closely with Percier and Fontaine, creating new designs to complement the new furniture of Jacob-Desmalter and Pierre-Benoit Marcion.

The designs of Neoclassical fabric, in contrast with those designed seventy-five years before, point out, more clearly perhaps than any other aspect of this style, the great difference between the elaborate movement of the baroque and the simple, almost thoughtful pace of Neoclassicism. These Neoclassical motifs were the ideal patterns for woven fabrics, since, on the whole, they were small, regular and easy to translate into woven terms. Not many of the silk mills, however, went as far as the famous cotton toile company at Jouy. Started in 1760 by C. P. Oberkampf, who both ran and designed for the factory, *toiles de Jouy* were and are at once recognizable by their elaborate monochrome prints, depicting everything from fairy tales to mythology, all reproduced in intricate detail due to the invention of copperplate printing. They were immediately popular, and Jean-Baptiste Huet designed many classical, and later Neoclassical, designs, several of which featured Napoleon on his many military campaigns. These so pleased the Emperor that he had the inside of his campaign tent hung with one—presumably a design that commemorated one of his victories.

The influence of the Empire extended to French tapestry makers too, and the factories at Beauvais and Gobelins used classical stories and Pompeiian borders on everything from portières to screens, wall-hangings to carpets.

Below: *One of four magnificent sofas designed by Robert Adam for Kedleston Hall, Derbyshire. The fine silk upholstery—in cerulean blue—dominates, set off by the splendid ormolu arms and feet carved in the shape of sporting sea gods, sea nymphs and fish.*

'Saturn', a carpet designed by Claude Audran le Jeune, and woven in silk and wool at the Gobelins factory outside Paris. The mythological subject is shown garnered with Neoclassical ornament, and a border designed to resemble a cornice.

The Sèvres Egyptian service, which was commissioned by Napoleon and given, by him, to Wellington after the battle of Waterloo. Egyptian motifs and decoration became very fashionable during the Napoleonic period, mostly as a result of his successful Egyptian campaign. Applied in a similar style they were evidently seen as an extension of Greek art.

Designs for vases made at the Sèvres factory, in the late eighteenth century. The shapes closely echo classical pottery, and the designs are taken from wall decorations found in excavations.

SÈVRES, THE ROYAL PORCELAIN FACTORY

It was important to Napoleon, from both a prestigious and economic point of view, that France and her products should continue to lead European taste. He took positive action with several of the best companies in an effort to give economic stability back to a country that had suffered so much from both war and revolution. Industry—whether fabric, porcelain or furniture—had not to be allowed to fail, and indeed Napoleon's commissions were given as much to keep the concerns going as to spread the word of Neoclassicism. In the event it did both. An example of this was the finely decorated porcelain wares from Sèvres, the French royal porcelain manufactory. Seen the world over as another sign of the superiority of French decorative talents, Sèvres porcelain was remarkable for the depth of ground colour that could be achieved, including the instantly recognizable deep blue, an inimitable turquoise and a warm deep pink—all of which are still admired today. But like the silk houses, Sèvres, too, after fifty years of success, went into decline during the years of the Revolution. In 1793 the factory had been nationalized, and then once Napoleon commissioned from them the Egyptian Service, among others, Sèvres confidently embraced the Neoclassical style. Not content with merely painting the china with Neoclassical scenes, the factory began to produce vases, ewers and other vessels shaped like newly found classical wares. With their rows of gilding and strong colours, Sèvres porcelain of the early nineteenth century exemplified the Empire and its decoration.

THE OUTPUT OF JOSIAH WEDGWOOD

Although the English equivalent of Sèvres was thought by many people to be Wedgwood, the company's beginnings and organization were very different. Josiah Wedgwood (1730–95) was an important influence on the spread of Neoclassical taste. He kept his product in front of the eyes of an admiring audience through constant experimentation with new processes and finishes, and consequently his business flourished throughout the eighteenth century.

Wedgwood left school at age nine, and at the age of eleven was a thrower at his brother Thomas's pottery works in Burslem. Starting on his own in 1759, he decided to keep an experiment book, wherein he wrote down his attempts to perfect different glazes. In 1765 he produced the best creamware yet seen, and in 1767 he perfected a fine black stoneware called basalt. For Neoclassical works, he wanted a body that seemed polished and cold—and like the vases of Antiquity, a simulation of marble or stone. Seven years after introducing his black basalt, he perfected a new flat stoneware that could be stained in colours, 'through its whole surface'. Perfect for Neoclassical ornament, the medium could be used to make everything from portrait busts to plant pots. The eminent Neoclassical sculptor John Flaxman was asked to provide designs, and Wedgwood searched for subjects in the collecting cabinets of his patrons, including Sir William Hamilton, now returned from his stint as British Envoy at Naples. So involved was Wedgwood with classicism that he called his china works, which he opened in 1769, Etruria. One of Wedgwood's best-known pieces is his ceramic copy of the Portland Vase; an outstanding example of Roman glass bought by Hamilton in Italy in 1783 and sold to the Dowager

Entitled, 'Female flute player: such as went about playing at entertainments. From a vase in my possession', this drawing by Thomas Hope was typical, not only of his interest in acquiring Greek antiquities, but also of his desire to educate.

A ceramic reproduction of the Portland Vase, modelled by Henry Webber, and made by Josiah Wedgwood in black jasperware. He developed this stoneware, which was first introduced in 1775, specifically for such work.

Duchess of Portland a year later. Made of black jasperware with white relief figures, the vase was drawn by William Hackwood and modelled by Henry Webber; its first edition dated to 1790–93.

Unlike many other manufacturers of the time, Wedgwood wanted to sell abroad. Small ornamental plaques were exported to France and, interested and excited by the French Revolution, he produced two commemorative medallions in jasperware. He worked hard on exporting his goods, and eventually secured the order for the famous Frog Service from Catherine the Great of Russia. The service was completed in 1775 and comprised 952 items, painted with 1,244 scenes. Not surprisingly, the service was expensive—as was all Wedgwood china. In the 1770s, Mrs Delany went to Christie's, where some pieces were displayed, and reported that Wedgwood's ware '. . . bears a price only for those who have superfluous money.' But although (and also probably because) they were expensive, they were deeply desirable, and Wedgwood's constant introduction of new ideas and products ensured a never-ending stream of visitors to his shop.

Below: 'The Choice of Hercules' was designed by the sculptor John Flaxman for Josiah Wedgwood as a suitably Neoclassical subject for one of the latter's popular plaques.

Jasperware, as produced by Josiah Wedgwood, took relief figures well, and Neoclassical scenes on vases such as this one, with a design by John Flaxman, were instantly popular.

MATTHEW BOULTON'S METALWORK

Wedgwood was a friend of Matthew Boulton (1728–1809), who worked with cut steel, among other materials. Boulton was a perfect product of the new breed of working man. His company, Boulton and Fothergill, which he started in 1761 at Soho, in Handsworth near Birmingham, not only developed Sheffield plate, but also silver and ormolu, for which the Adam brothers supplied him with designs. He also worked with James Watt on the development and patent of the steam engine.

Boulton's factory must have been huge. The ever-interested William Hugh Dalton said that it was made up of 'four squares, with shops, warehouses, etc,' for a thousand workmen who not only made buttons, buckles, boxes and trinkets in gold, silver and compositions, but 'in many other arts, long predominant in France which lose their reputation on a comparison with the product of this place'. Not only were there Boulton's men working on his concerns in the complex, there were also 'Mr Clay's japanning, Mr Taylor's buttons, and Mr Ray's whipmaking'.

Dalton further commented on the machines and their handsome output, noting

> The number of ingenious mechanical devices they avail themselves of, by the means of water mills. The plated work has the appearance of solid silver. Their excellent ornamental pieces have been admired by the nobility and gentry. Some articles lately executed in silver paste show that taste and elegance of design prevail here in a superior degree, and are with mechanism and chemistry happily united.

Interestingly, with the first gasp of the Industrial Revolution, came the first breath of industrial espionage. In Dalton's words:

> Without a letter of recommendation from some correspondent or person known at the manuractory, a stranger will find it difficult to get admittance. This caustion is not improper as persons have been known to visit the manufactories . . . with a view of obtaining particular information.

Left: *Venus clock-case made by Matthew Boulton at his foundry in Birmingham, around 1771. Influenced by Robert Adam, from whom he also commissioned designs, Boulton used ornament with a fine sense as to its application. His manufactory produced not only silver, but Sheffield plate, ormolu and cut steel.*

This vase of classical shape painted with a view of Malvern Priory from the firm of Worcester, Flight and Barr, is typical of later Neoclassical ceramics.

DECORATION IN SCANDINAVIA

Scandinavian Neoclassical decoration was also much lighter in tone, although in the beginning it was much influenced by French taste. Jean-Louis Desprez (1743–1804), who had spent some time in Italy, after winning the Grand Prix de Rome, and who had worked with de Wailly in Paris, started to work for Gustav III of Sweden from 1784, remaining there until his death. His designs were eclectic and combined elements from various sources, including Egypt and Greece. Another Frenchman who influenced Swedish taste was Louis-Adrien Masreliez (1748–1810), who was born in Paris but lived in Stockholm from the time he was five. When he was twenty-one, he travelled south, spending eight years in Rome. He returned to Stockholm in 1783, after which he received numerous commissions from Gustav III, including the Pavilion at Haga. It was distinguished for its plethora of Neoclassical detail, always applied with a light touch.

AMERICAN INTERIORS: THE FEDERAL STYLE

In the young American nation the ideas behind Neoclassicism, and the essential simplicity of Palladian architecture, were ones to which the founding fathers and their descendants could easily relate. Not for them the frivolity of the rococo or the majesty of the baroque. What little conscious design there was in the homes of the first settlers was proscribed very much by the materials readily available, as there was little manufacturing, and therefore little choice. Walls were wood-panelled, floors were wooden boards. Initially, decorating ideas came directly from Europe, particularly Britain. After the Revolution of 1776, however, England's influence waned.

American interiors then became more sophisticated and, more importantly, unique, but characterized by a simplicity that evaded many of their European counterparts. Classical motifs were still used, but always simplified, sometimes to the point of naivety. Excess was not in fashion, and ornamental additions, such as gilding, stucco and marble, were used sparingly. The arrangement and design of rooms became less primitive and lighter in tone, and the panelling was now painted, usually in a soft, pale colour, such as cream.

Left and detail above: *The King's Divan at the Haga Pavilion in Sweden, commissioned by Gustav III from Louis-Adrien Masreliez. A French designer, Masreliez had used his time in Rome in the 1770s to perfect a light decoration which he used to great effect in Sweden in the 1780s.*

The parlour at Deer Park, Baltimore, built around 1800. The influence of the Neoclassical can be seen, but treated in a wholly American way. Wall niches hold flowers instead of statues, and walls, floor and furniture are all light in tone.

The Cabinet Room at Thomas Jefferson's home, Monticello. Jefferson was able to indulge, both inside and out, his knowledge and love of the classical, as is shown by the Roman decorative arched doorway.

As time passed, American architects formulated and published their own ideas. From Thomas Jefferson at Monticello, where his involvement with the design of the interior went as far as designing a parquetry floor, to the later work of Benjamin Latrobe in the early 1800s, who, like earlier English architects, designed the furniture for his new houses, interior design and arrangement developed into what is now known as the Federal style. Beholden to neither the English nor the French, Federal interiors featured a simple pleasing classical line that bespoke America. Certain elements of Federal design, however, were borrowed from the repertoire of restrained motifs of both the Regency and the Empire. Fireplaces, doors and windows were surrounded by flat-surfaced simple pilaster forms, floors were often painted or polished, and curtains, when they were used at all, were often unadorned. It was a unique expression of the Neoclassical ideal.

The drawing room of the Pingree House in Salem, Massachusetts, designed by Samuel McIntire. Neoclassical motifs such as swags, urns and columns are used in a simple manner, very different in tone from European interiors.

incorporated both a frame for embroidery and a bag for equipment; drawing tables with adjustable easels; folding card tables; elaborate tea trays; conversation chairs; and strangely divided confidante sofas. Invented necessities like candle and urn stands, hanging shelves and brackets for busts, all helped to fill any extra space.

In the well-equipped dining room there were sideboards and tables, knife cases (often shaped like urns), cellarets and—from Sheraton in particular—mahogany bottle vases. The bedroom, too, could now boast no end of essential devices: bed stairs, pot cupboards (or night tables, as they were more delicately called), commodes, basin stands (made to stand in corners or against a wall), shaving tables, dressing glasses and well-stocked dressing boxes for travelling.

An all-over decorated chess table inlaid with busy scenes, typical of the new designs produced to fill the demand for leisure pursuits in the late eighteenth century.

A pedestal and urn, one of a pair, designed to stand either side of the dining room sideboard at Harewood House, Yorkshire, made by Thomas Chippendale around 1770.

A longcase clock in oak and mahogany by B. Bernadromes with case by C. L. Clare, and painted by Albert Mathias. Neoclassical influences can be seen both in the mythological painting of Pegasus and Andromeda, and the columns on face and case, as well as the pediment.

INCREASING INFORMALITY

All this domestic activity meant that, for many people, life had taken on a greater degree of informality. Rooms became littered with the hobbies of the moment, and chairs were used in far freer groupings, often placed in the centre of the room, at least during the day, rather than ranked in guardsman rows around the side of the room, as had been common earlier in the century.

In an age when Everyman wished to be known as a gentleman and the pursuit of status and fashionable acceptability was a way of life for many, it was not surprising that with something as relatively cheap as furniture (relative, that is to a completely new house), there would be more than one style that would be considered fashionable at any one time. New designs, whether formal or not, followed several themes, not just the Neoclassical. Some were based on medieval Gothic architecture, some inspired by the Western view of the exotic East, particularly the art of China, and much continued in the traditional way, following the French style, as it had done for centuries.

But Neoclassical was the one style that appealed to the innovators, the men of the Age of Enlightenment, who felt that truth lay with Ancient civilizations. Gothic was traditional English, with the style ever present in cathedrals all over Britain, and chinoiserie appeared to many another form of the rococo, and therefore lightweight. The classical alone seemed to have greater depths, and to lend itself to new design.

The best Neoclassical furniture was inspired by classical Greek and Roman forms, although as the Neoclassical period wore on, the designs became far removed from the early simple, subtle furniture of Ancient houses. As with most civilizations where life is conducted in the open air, there were, in Ancient Greece particularly, not many elaborate pieces but rather a few simple shapes that with time became even more refined.

CLASSICAL FURNITURE FORMS

Carved into stone mourning stelae, preserved in ash as at Pompeii and Herculaneum, and seen in some surviving wall-paintings, Greek and Roman furniture in its turn was often based on or influenced by the Egyptian. The early Greek couches on animal legs, for example, are very similar to pieces seen in Egyptian wall-paintings and within tombs. Turned legs also came from Pharaonic Egypt.

From the eighth century BC, couches with painted or carved rectangular supports and cut-out incisions were popular, these apparently a Greek innovation. Decorative motifs included the palmette and volute.

Much Neoclassical furniture was modelled on ancient Greek and ancient Egyptian examples, to be found in wall paintings and carved into stone. The production of this eighteenth-century Italian book plate was presumably in response to the demand for models to work from.

ΠΟΤΑΜΩΝΟΣ
ΤΩ ΛΕΣΒΟΝΑΚΤΟΣ
ΠΡΟΕΔΡΙΑ

Roman models too, more elaborate than Greek design, were much used; excavated frescoes gave detailed idea of what much Roman furniture looked like. Detail from an eighteenth-century Italian book plate.

Opposite: *Late eighteenth-century interior at Edgewater, a house overlooking the Hudson in New York State. Carefully restored to its original condition, this fine Neoclassical room combines a certain seriousness of demeanour with elegant proportions: the carpet is modern, but woven to an original design. The chairs are by Duncan Phyfe, the Scottish-born cabinetmaker who carried the Neoclassical furniture styles of Sheraton and others to America in 1792.*

Below left: *A Directoire stool made around 1810 with carved and giltwood legs in form of crossed sabres. It looks remarkably like its ancient ancestor, the diphros or backless stool.*

Several classical shapes were reproduced accurately during the 1700s. One was the *diphros*, a backless stool, forms of which can be seen at the Parthenon. Another often-replicated classical design, particularly in France during Napoleon's Empire period, was the throne shape, which originated in Egypt and became more refined in Greece, where it gained arm rails and decorative finials. Also invented by the Greeks was the *klismos*, a seat that was filled in with plaited thongs, stood on curving legs and had a gently rounded back that supported the sitter. This design, which was one of the most perfect ever created, has been used continuously ever since.

Over the centuries of classical civilization furniture designs changed, just as in architecture, with the Romans embellishing and ornamenting the original, simple forms with precious materials used as inlay and veneer, often creating objects of luxury rather than of simplicity.

EARLY FRENCH NEOCLASSICAL FURNITURE

The earliest identifiable Neoclassical furniture in Europe was probably designed by Louis-Joseph Le Lorrain around 1756, in Paris, for a room in Ange-Laurent Lalive de Jully's house. In 1740 Le Lorrain had gone to Italy, where he had stayed for eight years and where he became renowned for his designs for fantastic pyrotechnical displays for the French fireworks at the Festa della Chinea. After his return to Paris he was asked to design a suite of furniture for Lalive de Jully, a rich dilettante interested in antiquities, who had also commissioned Le Roy—the same Le Roy who had pre-empted Stuart and Revett in publishing the first studies of Greek antiquities—to create a study for him. This room, filled with Le Lorrain's strange furniture, ornamented with lions' heads and paws, initiated the craze for *le goût grec*, which swept Paris in the mid-eighteenth century.

To the French, used to furniture that was luxuriously comfortable, with swelling curves and confident lines, this style was unconventional, to say the least. Its lines were severe and without curves, and instead of gilded wings and feathers of ornament, they were bordered with austere, geometrical classical motifs. The differences between what had gone before and this new style were striking.

In England, too, the always avant-garde 'Athenian,' James Stuart, was following up his Greek-inspired garden temples as early as 1757, with pieces of furniture that looked distinctly classical, like the tripod for Lord Scarsdale at Kedleston and the furniture for the astonishing Painted Room at Spencer House in London.

A sofa, designed by James 'Athenian' Stuart as part of a set, for Spencer House in London. Revolutionary in its time, and in a style never before seen in London, the seats were based very much on the Grecian stone throne, but with infinitely more elaborate decoration, the frame itself resembling a winged lion-like creature.

Above: *Sphinx table by Giacomo Raffaelli (1743–1836) and Guiseppe Leonardi (fl. after 1781), gilt wood and inlaid specimen marble top. The sphinx in this elaborate piece of furniture is Greek, not Egyptian.*

ROBERT ADAM, PREMIER NEOCLASSICIST

But although these were important precursors of what was to come, it was, yet again, as with so much else in eighteenth-century decoration, Robert Adam who produced and popularized the best in the Neoclassical style in furniture. As with his interior decoration and his work on ceiling designs (see p.118), Adam was anxious to reflect the designs of the Ancients, rather than imitate them blindly.

Ceiling decoration on panels was often produced for Adam by Michelangelo Pergolesi, who in turn used such fine decorative artists as Angelica Kauffmann, Antonio Zucchi and Giambattista Cipriani. Because the whole of the design of the interior was looked on as one by Adam—essentially a modern view—much of his furniture design seemed to be influenced by, indeed often reflected, the original paintings on the ceilings, but intentionally so. The same *grotteschi* of Rome that had influenced his panel designs also influenced his furniture designs: 'that beautiful light style of ornament used by the ancient Romans'. Light in colour and tone, the furniture was austere in style, except for the decoration. Delicate classical motifs, which looked even lighter than on the originals, were carved or inlaid with honeysuckle, curved horned rams' heads, acanthus and medallion motifs. Chippendale worked with him at Kenwood and Harewood, and John Linnell was a collaborator at Osterley.

The lines of this new furniture must have been startling to those accustomed to the dark swirled, curved and gilded lines of early eighteenth-century furniture. As with his interiors, Adam did not pretend that he was re-creating classical Greek and Roman furniture—rather, he was using the themes and the influences, and wedding the best of the old to the best of the new. The result at its finest was a lightness and sophistication never seen before.

Left: *A satinwood cabinet for the Duchess of Manchester, designed by Robert Adam, to display some pietra dura panels, and made by Ince and Mayhew, with ormolu work by Matthew Boulton. Delicate inlay with Neoclassical motifs frame the cabinet, and the tapering legs are topped with Ionic capitals.*

Detail of a Thomas Chippendale dressing commode (see below), showing a complex design of marquetry, and a medallion of Diana framed within a laurel leaf, on ivory on a satinwood ground.

Dressing commode made by Chippendale for Harewood House in 1773. The innate craftsmanship behind the intricate concave panels and the complex delicate wreaths, could, in lesser hands, become heavy and overwrought.

CHIPPENDALE, HEPPLEWHITE AND SHERATON

Although neither Thomas Chippendale, George Hepplewhite nor Thomas Sheraton made furniture exclusively in the Neoclassical style, they are nevertheless the three best-known representatives of the cumulative genius of eighteenth-century cabinet-making. Between them, and over nearly a hundred years, they set the stamp on and standards for eighteenth-century English furniture, with designs that have been copied and imitated not only in Britain, but on the Continent and North America, too, for over 250 years.

The fame of these three design greats rests not only on the magnificence of their known extant pieces, but also on the fact that they all published catalogues or directories clearly illustrating designs for countless pieces, from urn stands to canopied beds, with accurate drawings of such details as

A satinwood standing bookcase and cupboard, made by Thomas Sheraton in 1800. Simpler in design than the work of his predecessor Chippendale, the lines of his furniture were often vertical but softened with oval decoration—all in fairly severe classical vein.

the reeding and fluting on legs and arms. These directories were subscribed to by cabinet-makers all over the country, and were used constantly as reference works. The styles of the three men differed enormously, however, reflecting the changes taking place in Neoclassical design as the century progressed.

Thomas Chippendale (1718–79) was born in Worcestershire, the son of a joiner. In the second part of the eighteenth century the centre of London's cabinet-making was Covent Garden, and it was there, in St Martin's Lane, where he set up his firm, Chippendale, Haig and Co. He published his designs in 1754 in *The Gentleman's and Cabinet Maker's Directory*, in whose preface he stated: 'I have given no design but what may be executed with advantage by the hands of a skilful workman.' Chippendale's works—whether in the French, Chinese or Gothic taste—were strong and sturdy, yet a new delicacy of line derived from earlier styles can be seen particularly in the work he did for Robert Adam. A man who was confident in his art, he also said in his preface: 'I am not afraid of the fate an author usually meets with on his first appearance, from a set of critics who are never wanting to shew their wit and malice on the performances of others.'

George Hepplewhite 'the Graceful' (d. 1786) produced furniture that incorporated the leitmotifs of Neoclassicism, but with an element of fantasy that was akin to the rococo. A shadowy personality, he did not publish his designs in his lifetime, though they were issued by Alice, his widow two years after his death. Of his characteristic trademarks, the shield back—sometimes filled with Prince of Wales' feathers, sometimes with urns or ears of wheat—is the most representative. Adam's influence is obvious and could be seen on knife cases, writing tables, even library bookcases.

Unlike Chippendale and Hepplewhite, Thomas Sheraton (1751–1806), who was born in Stockton-on-Tees, made furniture for relatively few years, instead concentrating on the production of design manuals, in particular *The Cabinet-Maker and Upholsterer's Drawing Book*, which was first issued in parts between 1791 and 1794. Thomas Sheraton was cognizant of his own talent, and in the preface to his *Drawing Book*, he presented a brief, if biased, résumé of earlier furniture directories. Many years had passed since Chippendale's first directory had been published, and Sheraton dismissed his predecessor's early designs as 'Wholly antiquated and laid aside, though possessed of great merit, according to the times in which they were executed.' Hepplewhite, too, fared badly in Sheraton's estimation:

> Some of these designs are not without merit, though it is evident that the perspective is, in some instances, erroneous. But ... if we compare some of the designs, particularly the chairs, with the newest taste, we shall find that this work has already caught the decline, and, perhaps, in a little time will suddenly die in the disorder.

The lines of Sheraton's furniture were vertical, their motifs were classical and the manner in which he combined the two possessed great style and charm. His undoubted talent, although recognized and commended, nevertheless went unrewarded, and he died a poor man.

EBÉNISTES AND *MENUISIERS*

During the 1760s in France, there was no Robert Adam to swing the mood away from the traditional classical to a new look. Before the Revolution, the French—rather, the Parisians—those few hundred tastemakers who were still considered the arbiters of comfort and style, moved slowly towards a more Neoclassical look in furniture, although the new style was not to become popular until after the Revolution. As well as always having been more comfortable than English furniture, French pieces were also considerably more ornate. The French cabinet-maker who specialized in veneered work—or *ébeniste*, as he was known—relied heavily on craftsmen working in ormolu, porcelain and lacquer for the detailing on their furniture. The *menuisiers*, or makers of carved sofas, chairs and other

pieces worked very closely with the upholsterer, whose position in France was far greater than that of his equivalent in England. Towards the end of the century simpler lines started to appear, and several of the great furniture-makers who were to continue to work through the years of the Revolution, like Georges Jacob, introduced Pompeiian-inspired ornament into their designs.

The same Parisian house that Horace Walpole described as having a wall practically made of glass (p. 129), had much ornate furniture filling every room. He did not think any more highly of this than he had of the crystals and mirrors: 'Then you must stuff them [the rooms] fuller than they will hold, with granite tables and porphyry urns and bronzes, and statues and vases and the Lord or devil knows what.'

An inlaid writing table of rosewood, c. 1780, resembling a Louis XIV bonheur du jour. This classical piece may hark back 100 years, but it still makes concessions to the new Neoclassical style of decoration.

A marble and ormolu clock made in the late eighteenth century by French craftsman Pierre Philippe Thomire. Although Neoclassical in its subject matter, it is far more elaborate than its English counterpart would have been.

LESS DERIVATIVE ENGLISH FORMS

Meanwhile, in England, there was towards the end of the century a movement away from the word as spoken by Adam. Adam died in 1792, but before that Henry Holland, the architect who worked on Carlton House for the Prince of Wales, produced designs for furniture that, although still classical in content, seemed to owe more to the lines of original classical pieces than to Adam's light adaptations. The change had started with the later designs of Thomas Sheraton, wherein simple, rectilinear shapes decorated with both Greek and Egyptian classical motifs anticipated Regency furniture, although it was not for some time that furniture was to become directly derivative of classical design.

The intensity of feeling that was behind the entire Empire movement could never have been repeated in England. Although the country was at war for some of the period with Napoleon, life was still far more secure and safe in Britain than on the other side of the Channel. The catalyst for the new look, if such a thing was necessary, was the lifestyle of the Prince Regent, but much of the Regency style was simply a reaction against Adam and a natural progression of taste.

As in architecture itself, one of the chief protagonists of this change in style was Thomas Hope.

An ornamental cupboard by Jacob Frères with caryatids mounts by Thomire, massive and mighty in its combination of materials and ornament. Jacob Frères used many different master craftsmen in the execution of their cabinet work.

Right: *English hall seat of beech painted to imitate grey veined white marble in 1800. The design was inspired by an illustration of a classical Roman seat that had been published in 1799 by C. H. Tatham.*

A Trafalgar chair, c. 1810, designed after the battle of Trafalgar with the back rails supposedly representing pieces of rope, to convey a suitably nautical image.

An Abbotsford chair. This early nineteenth-century chair was based on Greek classical designs but tempered by the fluid lines of Regency style.

Below: *An English Regency sofa with scroll ends and cane seat. It differs from what had gone before in its close resemblance to a Grecian couch. It is simpler by far in both concept and decoration than its French cousin, the Empire sofa.*

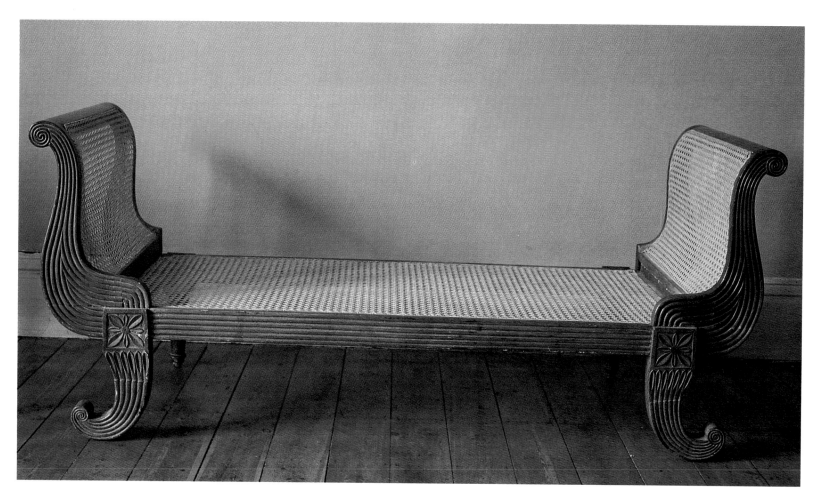

THOMAS HOPE'S INFLUENCE

Thomas Hope's passion for classical authenticity in furniture (see p. 134) was popularized by cabinet-maker George Smith. Smith published *Collection of Designs for Household Furniture and Interior Decoration* in 1808 in order to appeal to the growing middle-class market, and to the new furniture factories.

The woods used, too, had changed from Adam's day. The relative simplicity of the new designs called for dark, shining surfaces, such as those of rosewood, mahogany and exotic varieties, like zebra wood.

Some designs popularized then have become instantly recognizable as products of the Regency. The Trafalgar chair, with its ropelike back, many examples of which are still to be found (see p. 168), and the classical sofa, with its scrolled Grecian ends and firm upholstered seat, epitomize the grace of this period. A few years later, however, this simplicity was lost. Excess ornament was applied, curves appeared where none had been before and the elegance of Regency furniture was gone.

A typically complex and ornate mahogany secretaire made for the Imperial Russian court by David Roentgen, a German cabinet maker who, from his workshop at Neuwied, made pieces for many of the courts of Europe.

FURNITURE IN RUSSIA

The fine new palaces built by Catherine the Great and Alexander I needed a great deal of furniture, and much of it was bought on travels and commissioned through agents living abroad. Some was purchased by Catherine from the German David Roentgen (1743–1807), who spent much of his time travelling around Europe selling his designs. Roentgen came to St Petersburg in 1783, having already achieved fame in Paris for his furniture, which he designed himself and made in his factory in Neuwied. Soon, Russian craftsmen began to make furniture as fine as many of the imported pieces, and distinctive in its own right.

Charles Cameron, too, Catherine's Scottish-born architect, designed and commissioned specific pieces for the Empress, particularly for the rooms he designed at Tsarskoe Selo. Neoclassically inspired, Cameron's furniture nevertheless was richer than anything being designed in England or France at the time and was as heavy and ornate as his interior decors.

Russian architects like Zakharov and Voronikhin, who rebuilt Pavlovsk after the war with Napoleon, also began to design furniture. Their work followed very closely the later antique styles of England and France, but possessed a characteristic Russian richness.

A malachite urn with gilt bronze mounts, made in Russia around 1810. Russian taste demanded a suitably opulent and exotic look, and much use was made of semi-precious stones.

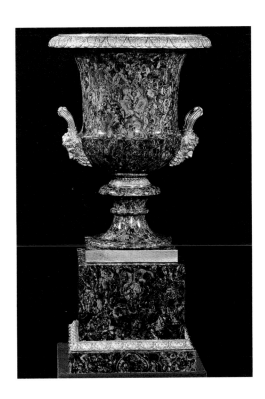

THE SCANDINAVIAN LIGHT TOUCH

In Scandinavia, Neoclassicism was tempered with an already clearly discernible predilection for lightness of touch. Carl Gustav III, a declared Francophile, brought Parisians Louis-Adrien Masreliez and Jean-Louis Desprez to Sweden. As well as creating the decoration for the pavilion at Haga, Masreliez produced its furniture, in a style that combined Neoclassical motifs with an almost rococo feel. In Denmark, the new Academy in Copenhagen became a centre for Neoclassical design under the leadership of Jacques-François Saly. The Empire style later was adopted in Scandinavian furniture, but again with a lightness and taste that often was not evident elsewhere.

GERMAN AND AUSTRIAN FURNITURE

When not selling his furniture to monarchs like Catherine of Russia, David Roentgen was producing Neoclassical designs in his factory at Neuwied in the 1770s and 1780s, but it was not until the turn of the century, and the emergence of the Empire style, that Neoclassical furniture became popular. But as with other aspects of interior design (see p. 146) it was a very different Empire style to that of France, with no dark, heavy woods finished with ormolu or gilt. In Germany and Austria the new style made use of light woods and simple, classical shapes, the outlines of which were often plainly delineated with ebony banding.

FURNITURE IN THE NEW WORLD

Before the American Revolution, well-made contemporary English furniture was shipped to the colonies, where it was often copied by skilled cabinet-makers. But far more influential, at least in the second part of the eighteenth century, were the directories produced by that trio of great furniture designers, Chippendale, Hepplewhite and Sheraton. The colonists of the New World could build their furniture in the manner of the Old, but as with everything else, with their own distinctive variations. Copies were not required, adaptations were.

By the mid-1700s there were many highly skilled cabinet-makers in America, and furniture had reached a high level of sophistication. It was being made in cities up and down the length of the Eastern seaboard, and after the end of the war with England in 1783, the Federal style—the American interpretation of Neoclassicism—was born. Like American architecture at this time, Federal furniture took from, but did not directly copy, the styles of the Old World. Emigrés included craftsmen from every Euoropean country, each adding their own particular heritage to their creations.

A scroll-back side chair made of mahogany in 1807 by Duncan Phyfe's workshop in New York City. Son of an emigrant Scot, Phyfe, who employed over a hundred craftsmen, based much of his work on the earlier designs of Sheraton, although the finished piece is totally American in look.

An armchair by John and Hugh Findlay of Baltimore, heavy with the sort of inlay work that was a trademark of the city. Baltimore furniture-makers were known for their fine handling of ornament and decoration on their cabinet work.

THE MANY FACETS OF THE FEDERAL STYLE

The Federal style was not a single style but many distinctive ones, each based in and around a particular city. Important centres of cabinet-making included New York, Philadelphia and Boston, and work from each city was easily recognizable to the knowledgeable.

The Boston style tended to be plain and massive, with Neoclassical ornament applied in the guise of columns and pilasters. Typical of its adherents was Samuel McIntire (1757–1811). A woodcarver by trade, he taught himself architecture, and filled the houses he designed with much carved ornament to sit above mantels and doors. His furniture was simple, masculine and comfortable. John Seymour (1738–1818) was recognized as a cabinet-maker in England before he emigrated to America in 1785. With his son, Thomas, he began to make furniture in Boston, and their delicate pieces were often inspired by designs from both Sheraton and Hepplewhite.

New York, then fast growing in importance, was the base of Duncan Phyfe (1768–1854), an emigrant from Scotland. He had a large shop, employing more than a hundred craftsmen, where he made furniture that was often based on Sheraton's designs, although his interpretations of such pieces have a vigour and strength that is entirely American. His designs epitomized the Federal style: lighter than Empire, more assertive than Regency, with Neoclassical ornament used boldly but not to excess. French influence was brought to New York by the *ébéniste* Honoré Lannuier (1779–1819), who learned his craft in Paris. After his arrival in America in 1803, however, the Frenchman simplified the heavy tones of his native Empire style.

Cabinet-makers in the city of Baltimore were known by their mastery of fine ornamentation. Veneer and inlay became art forms there, as did glass inserts with reverse-side painting, often in recognizably Neoclassical gold and black, and depicting classical figures. Maryland cabinet-makers were also renowned for their writing desks and console tables, some pieces decorated with exquisite marquetry.

In Philadelphia, at one time America's largest city (and the nation's capital from 1790 to 1800), cabinet-makers like Dublin-born Joseph B. Barry and Thomas Wetherill produced designs that were still inspired by the simplicity and ideals of the early pioneers. Strong, simple bookcases and desks were designed with the minimum of ornament, and were often solely reliant on contrasting veneers for decoration.

Newport, Rhode Island, too, was an important cabinet-making city, with members of the large Townsend-Goddard dynasty producing pieces such as outstanding blockfront highboys, with the front divided into three sections, the central one slightly recessed. Also from Townsend-Goddard came lowboys, secretaries, desks and bureaux. The family were known especially for their distinctive carved-shell motifs, a regional variation on a Neoclassical device which they employed in both its concave and convex forms, and which seemed to decorate every one of their designs.

VII

THE
NEOCLASSICAL
GARDEN

PRESENT-DAY KNOWLEDGE OF ANCIENT GARDENS is not extensive. There is little record of the part gardens played in the lives of the Greeks, although it is known that vegetables were cultivated, and holy sites were chosen for their natural beauty. There does not seem to be much evidence of the pleasure garden in Greece, however—at least not the sort of fabled terraced gardens designed in Persia and other countries of the East.

Practical gardens were much in evidence, however, for a great deal of Ancient Greek life was conducted out of doors, resulting in such places as the Groves of Academe, now embedded in cliché but originally the gardens of Academia in Athens. Shade was at a premium in Mediterranean Greece, and arbours and walks and perambulating places hung with trees were grown in large cities. In the precincts of private houses, temples and shrines often were erected in garden-like areas.

The gardens of Stourhead, with the Pantheon prominent across the lake. Easily seen from the surrounding countryside, it symbolizes the classical ideal, important to the eighteenth century Neoclassical garden.

TOWN AND COUNTRY GARDENS

The Romans appear to have had a much more relaxed approach to gardens, and many more citizens had private ones. Just as today, there seemed to be two sorts of private gardens: the town variety, usually set within the surrounds of the house, and the country type, where there were no restrictions of space. Among the excavated houses at Herculaneum and Pompeii are several town villas with the remains of very sophisticated gardens within the peristyle. Some of these were paved, others had intricate mosaic floors and many were furnished with statuary and relief sculptures set against the walls. There were rooms opening off the court, which was sometimes edged by a colonnade, and often there was water—reflecting in a pool or stone bowl, or cascading in a fountain.

The gardens of country villas, where land was close to boundless, were quite different. Hadrian's famous villa outside Rome boasted gardens that stretched for acres, incorporating water, colonnades, columns and trees. And such gardens were not just natural landscapes using the indigenous flora. The Romans spent much time on the cultivation and care of plants and trees, as shown by Pliny the younger when describing one of his much-loved gardens at his villa in Tuscany.

Topiary was already popular and well developed as an art, and Pliny wrote not only of box hedges clipped into different shapes, but also of a bank lined on each side with animals made from box. The entire garden was enclosed by a stone wall shielded from the house by yet another clipped box hedge, this one planted and cut in rising tiers. The use of clipped trees and formal hedging to delineate spaces makes this garden sound much like the forerunner of sixteenth-century Italian and French formal gardens.

THE ROLE OF WATER IN ROMAN GARDENS

Water, too, was used extensively in the Roman garden, whether in fountains, simple pools or basins. In the same Tuscan house and garden, Pliny described a small courtyard with a fountain in a marble basin, a room with an internal fountain and, in front of the house, an ornamental pool with its own waterfall. At Hadrian's Villa, the garden seems to have been designed around water, used not only for its beauty and cooling properties, but also as an architectural element, with statues and buildings placed at strategic points to be reflected or emphasized by the curves of water. But they did not simply use water as ornament. They employed their considerable engineering skills to utilize fully their supplies, building not only thermal baths, but swimming baths too, and diverting water sources into specially constructed channels to irrigate their land.

And, of course, there were flowers—jasmine, roses, violets and oleander—and Pliny wrote of beds of acanthus. Fruit trees grew in abundance: citrus fruits like orange and lemon, as well as mulberry and fig.

ROME'S SACRED LANDSCAPES

Extant fragments of paintings show the Roman 'sacred landscape.' This was a special place dedicated to a god, the whole usually set in a carefully chosen, naturally beautiful spot, so that people might walk about in serenity. The area was enhanced by a small temple or grotto, and small trees were planted to give some light shade.

The fall of the Roman Empire meant the fragile and transient beauty of these cultivated gardens were trampled underfoot, and they returned to the wilderness, leaving little if anything for later archaeologists to examine.

The Canopus at Hadrian's villa at Tivoli, where porticoes, promenades and pavilions were reflected by water from lakes, pools and fountains. Statues and sculpture were everywhere, creating a model much followed in the eighteenth century.

The garden frescoes from the Villa of Livia in Rome. The Romans cultivated many different shrubs and trees, including citrus fruits.

RENEWED INTEREST IN THE RENAISSANCE

With the wealth and stability of the Renaissance, and the new villas of Florentine and Roman nobles, came a resurgence of the grand garden, many built and planted in much the same places as their Antique ancestors. They existed on the hills outside the cities and indeed within the cities themselves, such as the villa and garden of Innocent VIII, who was Pope from 1484 to 1492; built just north of the Vatican, the villa featured, along with its garden, a green inner courtyard that displayed great excavated treasures.

Of course, eighteenth-century Neoclassical gardens could never have been accurate copies of the Antique. There was little classical antecedent, and by and large new gardens, no matter how unsuited to the setting, followed the formal gardens of the Renaissance, which had been and were still being created in France and Italy.

Andrea Palladio, so often the source for classical reference, printed few words on landscaping direction. He did not, on the whole, design gardens to go with his classical country villas on the Veneto, for the original structures he created were designed to integrate, as far as possible, with the cultivated land around them.

THE EVOLUTION OF THE NEOCLASSICAL GARDEN

The formal, classical garden had never had such a hold in England as in France and Italy. On the Continent, since the time of the Renaissance, there had been a tradition for grand gardens, the design of which was often entrusted to architects, and which enhanced and underlined the importance of the house with elaborate constructions of masonry or planting. Yet it was evident to eighteenth-century architects, particularly in England, that the simple, solid Palladian-inspired villas they were being asked to re-create all over the countryside needed gardens that complemented the houses, not fought against them. The intricacies of the formal garden—the *allées*, the clipped box, the geometric formality—seemed artificial, and too fussy for the elegant, simple, yet imposing structure of these houses. Politically, too, the climate had changed, and the concepts of free thought and the rise of the middle classes were reflected, as with houses, in a greater simplicity.

Thus developed the Neoclassical garden, something entirely new in the history of cultivated gardens and part of a wider landscape movement, where straight lines were banished and all appeared to grow naturally.

Landscape Near Rome with a View of the Ponte Molle, *by Claude Lorraine (1600-1682). Claude's pastoral paintings were to have a large influence on gardens and gardeners of the eighteenth century.*

PAINTINGS INFLUENCE GARDENS

In Europe, artists like Claude and Nicolas Poussin were painting idealized Antique landscapes through which thinking men strolled in harmony with nature. This, then, was the key, and the Neoclassical garden was to be like a painting. The perfect garden would contrast light with shade and shadow with luminescence; trees would be planted in artful groups, to give definition to and to enhance the buildings, either set behind them or used as signposts towards them. The landscape was a garden, and the garden a landscape, either natural or man-made.

The owners of the new eighteenth-century English houses, were equally interested in their gardens: Lord Cobham at Stowe, Lord Lyttleton at Hagley, Lord Burlington at Chiswick and at Syon the Duke of Northumberland, who took great interest in rural architecture and was involved enough to design his own greenhouse.

SERPENTINE WATER

Water was vital to these new gardens as well. But it was, as Horace Walpole put it, 'Adieu to canals, circular basins, and cascades tumbling down marble steps.' The new way to use water was not in the old, formal manner, but so that it curved or, as they might have said, 'serpentized'.

Indeed, the word 'serpentine' was used constantly during the eighteenth century to describe water in a landscape. In rather cavalier fashion, these early garden makers diverted, constructed and altered the course of water to give them the required serpentizing effect. According to Walpole, William Kent was the master of water, and one of the main features of Lord Burlington's garden at Chiswick, which he and Kent created together, was the serpentine river that gave form to the garden. At Syon, too, the grounds were altered by the creation of an artificial serpentine river, which cut the land into two separate parts and ran down to join the Thames.

Where there was water there could, of course, be bridges. Never far from sight, Palladio's influence crept in here, and bridges built to his designs rose in gardens from Wilton to Stowe and Stourhead to Hagley, even at Catherine the Great's palace at Tsarskoe Selo in Russia.

As the Neoclassical garden developed, it seemed to become a symbolic entity, wherein allegory was rife. Avenues, paths, temples, seats—all were given meaningful names, although whether a meaning only in the garden architect's eye or a deeper one was not always apparent. Buildings were also designed as symbols, both to engender thought and discussion, and with a more practical purpose: to show off a vista or some other significant point the designer felt the viewer should see, by giving it a strong and imposing focal point.

The Palladian bridge at Wilton House, one of the earlier interpretations of Palladian bridges that were to appear in gardens all over England.

STOWE, THE PINNACLE
OF EARLY NEOCLASSICISM

The garden at Stowe epitomized many of these ideals. Called at the time a 'place so completely calculated to inform the judgement and indulge the fancy; where art appears without affectation, and nature without extravagance,' it was perhaps the earliest great Neoclassical garden in England—and therefore in Europe, since the landscape garden originated in England, rather than, as usual, in Italy or France.

Viscount Cobham (1675–1738) started working on Stowe, which he had inherited, in about 1713. He planned it with the help of Charles Bridgeman—already well known as a gardener—who supposedly invented, and introduced at Stowe, the ha-ha, the garden device that did more than any other to initiate the new landscaped garden, obviating as it did the need for what were seen at the time as artificial boundaries. John Vanbrugh, a friend of Lord Cobham, designed some buildings for Stowe's grounds, and over the next twenty years the garden was extended in all directions.

After Bridgeman's death, William Kent was asked to design more buildings for Stowe, as well as to work on its garden, specifically to construct something new to replace the Oriental garden, by now a spent fashion. He set to work with, as Walpole put it, 'the pencil of his imagination,' and designed the valley known as the Elysian Fields, where attempts were made to re-create the idea of a quasi-religious feeling—in essence, the sacred landscape—and indeed the buildings and areas were given names.

Stowe's garden at this time must have been an amazing sight. The temples alone—several of them designed by James Gibbs, architect of the church of St-Martin-in-the-Fields—merit detailed examination. There was one to Friendship and another one to Concord and Victory, one dedicated to Bacchus, and another to Venus, and one of Gothic mien. The temple of Ancient Virtue faced that 'well known satire', the instant ruin of the Temple of Modern Virtue. There was also a shepherd's cave, the Corinthian arch, an Egyptian pyramid and an Italian belvedere. Statues lined the paths, and the requisite Palladian bridge spanned the water, apparently based on that at Wilton. At the head of the water was a grotto of shells where Earl Temple (Lord Cobham's successor, who inherited Stowe in 1749) would sometimes dine, looking out over the lake, which was illuminated in the evenings. The different areas of the garden were connected by a circuit walk which wound around the irregular lake and was designed to afford fine views at many points. Capability Brown became head gardener here in 1741, many years after the gardens had been laid out by Bridgeman.

The Temple of British Worthies at Stowe, the truly vast landscape park created and refined by three great English landscape designers—Charles Bridgeman, William Kent and Lancelot 'Capability' Brown. At Stowe, 'temples' by Kent and Vanbrugh, emphasizing the stern virtues of past ages, are set amid an arcadian landscape of lakes and vistas.

The Temple of Ancient Virtue, at Stowe by William Kent, was designed as a classical temple, and unlike the Temple of Modern Virtue was naturally complete in all respects.

179

THE GENIUS OF WILLIAM KENT

Horace Walpole, among others, considered that of all his skills, gardening was the greatest talent possessed by William Kent. Speaking about the gradual development of the garden away from an intensely formal arrangement, Walpole said: 'At that moment appeared Kent, painter enough to taste the charms of landscape, bold and opinionative enough to dare and dictate, and born with a genius to strike out a great system from the twilight of imperfect essays.'

During the time Kent was designing Stowe, he was also laying out the gardens at Claremont for the Duke of Newcastle and Carlton House for the Prince of Wales. The most complete Kent-designed garden that remains today is the one at Rousham in Oxfordshire, which General James Dormer commissioned him to design in 1737, and of which it was said, on completion, 'the whole is as elegant and antique as if the Emperor had selected that most pleasing solitude'.

CHISWICK AND STOURHEAD

One of the earliest gardens Kent worked on, in around 1733, was that of his mentor and patron, Lord Burlington. At Burlington's house at Chiswick, he and Kent altered the original gardens, with Kent's skills greatly in evidence. The river, spanned by a wooden, Palladian-inspired bridge, serpentized through the garden, at the end of which was a Roman temple and an obelisk with grass slopes. In the centre of this was a circular piece of water. A path led to a wilderness, through which were three straight avenues terminated by three different structures.

Later than Stowe, but just as famous and beautiful, were the gardens of Stourhead in Wiltshire, which were created by that house's owner, Henry Hoare. Stourhead itself was a Palladian house, and the grounds were laid out from about the 1740s as a picturesque garden. Considered by many the summation of all English Neoclassical gardens, Stourhead boasts a famous garden view where a Pantheon, designed by Henry Flitcroft after the Roman original, sits across the lake, and which includes not only Neoclassical figures, but also an Antique marble figure brought back from Herculaneum.

CAPABILITY BROWN'S 'LANDSKIPS'

No story of Neoclassical gardening would be complete without mention of Lancelot 'Capability' Brown (1715–83). Although he was not, in the strictest sense, part of the Neoclassical movement, he was much influenced by Kent, with whom he worked at Stowe, and also, with his enthusiasm for landscaping, or landskips, continued the idea of a garden as a painting, a place for the soul. Brown spent the major part of his working life during the first wave of Neoclassicism, employed by landowners like Lord Egremont at Petworth and Lord Cobham at Stowe, who were immersed in the style. After his work at Stowe in conjunction with William Kent, he began to remodel many of the great gardens of the time. He soon began to paint in grand strokes, changing the course and shape of rivers, making lakes where none stood before, removing buildings that obscured the new view and planting whole groves of trees to achieve his final aim: the perfect landscape garden, where every prospect pleases. Or, as Walpole said, 'That chief beauty of all gardens, prospect and view: we tire of all the painter's art when it wants these finishing touches.' For thirty years until his death, Capability Brown planned the gardens, and in some cases the houses, for many of the great estates of Britain, altering irrevocably the look of English landscape.

A summer-house with the motto Templa Quam Dilecta, the family motto of the owner of Stowe, Lord Temple.

Opposite: *The Italian Garden at Mount Edgcumbe, on the borders of Devon and Cornwall. Laid out in the early nineteenth century by Sir Richard Edgecumbe (1764–1839), the garden pleasingly combines classical elements from the Renaissance and the ancient world—including a Greek-revival fountain, and statues faithfully copied from originals in Italy.*

A view across the grounds of Blenheim Palace laid out by Capability Brown in the 1760s, and showing the bridge designed by Vanbrugh. It was intended to rise above a river but sits semi-submerged, as Brown altered the channel of the river to make a lake.

FOR EVERY GARDEN A TEMPLE

The Neoclassical garden was indeed the garden of the temple. These symbols of others' Antiquity, placed in an otherwise natural setting, were there both as things of beauty and focal points in a carefully planned landscape, but also as signposts or reminders, to make people stop, think and question. Many of the buildings designed and constructed in this period were copies of existing classical buildings, for here was the perfect opportunity for a well-travelled architect, fired with the experience of the Ancients, to re-create one of his inspirations—a miniature temple, tower, shrine or monument that he had so carefully measured and sketched during his time abroad. From William Kent, who turned garden temples into an art, to William Chambers, who re-created classically correct originals, to 'Athenian' Stuart, with his careful placing of hitherto unseen Greek temples at Hagley Hall—no garden was complete without its classical monument.

Stuart's gardens at Hagley Hall, home of the Lord Lyttelton, nephew of Lord Cobham at Stowe, were, in fact, famous in their own time, partially because of the copy of the Temple of Theseus, built in the grounds in 1758. As well as the famous temple there were statues, monuments, a pavilion, a ruin, a rotunda of Ionic order, a Palladian bridge, a root house, or hermitage, and, most unusual of all, a mock castle designed by Sanderson Miller.

WILLIAM SHENSTONE AND THE LEASOWES

But Hagley, and indeed possibly Stowe and Stourhead, seemed relatively simple in concept when compared to The Leasowes, the garden of a neighbour of Lord Lyttleton, William Shenstone (1714–63), the poet. In many ways The Leasowes seems to have been the epitome of Neoclassical gardening, and indeed it was famed during Shenstone's lifetime and afterwards, although it is unfortunately now destroyed (a golf club occupies the area today). (Horace Walpole, as sceptical as ever, thought that the desire for vicarious fame was the only reason that Shenstone had gone to the huge expense of creating it.)

By the time William Shenstone created his garden in the countryside outside Birmingham, between 1745 and 1763, it appeared that the tour of the garden enthusiast was to be an arduous, if mentally stimulating, task. The circuit of The Leasowes was a winding walk that held a treasure trove of inscriptions and poems, statues and urns. Every turn made in the garden brought with it surprises. As a poet, Shenstone lost no opportunity to create and communicate. Around every corner, by every view, almost on every tree trunk was a motto, an inscription or a poem—most with the purpose of making a moral or philosophical point, usually in conjunction with a classical or literary allusion. There are not many contemporary descriptions of this then renowned garden, but one appeared in *The New English Traveller*, a book published around 1796 and covering a 'highly pleasing variety of subjects'. The writer, William Hugh Dalton, devoted several thousand words to marvel about 'The Leasowes, the seat of the late ingenious William Shenstone Esq, who laid out the gardens in such a manner as to improve the beauties of nature, and render them the admiration of all who have had the pleasure of seeing them.'

THE FASHION FOR HERMITAGES

Altogether, Dalton counted 35 seats and benches, one grotto, one bower, two groves, one Gothic alcove, one temple of Pan and one roothouse at The Leasowes. Roothouses were sometimes used as hermitages. Whether the general interest in all things classical had anything to do with the emergence of the hermit in the fashionable garden is hard to know, but they did appear, and were sometimes written of in the Neoclassical garden. Charles Hamilton is said to have had one in his garden at Painshill, Surrey. A vagary of fashion, rather than a serious addition to the garden, the idea of a hermit and a hermitage was not universally admired even then; indeed, Walpole thought 'it almost comic to set aside a quarter of one's garden to be melancholy in'.

The creation of an eighteenth-century garden could quite literally turn the owner into a pauper. The same Charles Hamilton found that the garden he had acquired in 1738—which boasted Roman temples, a mausoleum and bath, and a grotto—used up his entire fortune. William Shenstone, too, owner of The Leasowes, died a poor man.

CHAMBERS AND KEW

William Chambers was a garden designer as well as an architect. In 1757 the then Prince of Wales commissioned him to lay out Kew as a Royal Garden. In his work there he embraced much of the current Neoclassical thinking. Three quarters of the estate at Kew was fields and only a small part garden, but by the time Chambers had finished with the project, temples and ornaments abounded, of which the rebuilt Temple to Bellona and Pan remains today.

The temple of Flora at Stourhead built in 1745, with an inscription from The Aeneid. *It was part of the planned circuit along which visitors would walk, stopping at specific spots to be elevated, elated or instructed.*

Colonnade from the Parc Monceau, Paris, laid out in 1773 as a French interpretation of an English garden. The garden had a number of diverse monuments that ranged from a Dutch windmill to a minaret.

THE JARDIN ANGLAIS

The landscape garden movement did not sweep Europe in the same way that Neoclassical architecture did. Traditionalists like Jean-François Blondel, author of the influential *Cours d'architecture*, praised the merits of the French formal garden against the *jardin anglais*. And there is no doubt that the structured formality of the French garden suited the equally structured formal houses well. Nevertheless, after the signing of the Anglo-French peace treaty in 1763, and again after the French Revolution, the idea of the English garden, complete with maximum numbers of 'folies', did become fashionable for a time. But rather than complete gardens in the English mode, the French often designed *jardins anglais* as adjuncts to the rest of the more formal garden. Within the *jardin anglais*, there might be monuments, temples, bridges and vistas.

The Anglophile Duc de Chartres began to plant his grand garden (designed by Carmontel, a writer and painter), the Parc Monceau, in 1773, some of which remains today. It contained a wood of tombs, temples, a pyramid and various other structures, some more Antique than others. Although called a *jardin anglais* by the French, the garden was considered by visiting English to retain its French formality. Bagatelle, the garden designed for the Comte d'Artois (later Charles X) by Thomas Blaikie (1758–1838), a Scottish gardener who spent much time working in France, was another creation that gave more than a passing nod to the conventions of the Neoclassical garden sarcophagus, mausoleum and Temple of Love.

But the purest Gallic manifestation of the *jardin anglais* was Ermenonville, in Oise, which was designed by the Marquis de Girardin in the 1760s and was much influenced by The Leasowes. Known as the place of Rousseau's burial—in the Île des Peupliers—Ermenonville revolves around a central and secondary axis, both filled with the variety of vistas, monuments, mottoes and inscriptions that gave pleasure to the lover of an eighteenth-century English garden.

RUSSIA'S GRAND GARDENS

Farther east, Catherine the Great of Russia thought about her gardens endlessly, as did many members of the Russian nobility. Now that her houses had been designed in the Neoclassical manner, the Tsarina instigated a Neoclassical garden at her palace at Tsarskoe Selo. She sent her landscape artist Vasily Neyelov to England in around 1770, and he stayed there for six months studying the English garden. John Busch, too, another English landscape gardener, went to Russia towards the end of the eighteenth century at Catherine's behest, to advise her at Pulkova and then at Tsarskoe Selo. As with architecture in Russia, it was very fashionable at the time to have a garden that had been laid out in a suitably classical way by one of the recognized artist-gardeners. Charles Cameron, who had been working for Catherine on both the interior decoration of the palace at Tsarskoe Selo and extensions to it, was responsible for some of the planning and design work in its gardens. He provided a pavilion or two and two Chinese bridges, although they were not strictly Neoclassical, and at Pavlosk, home of Catherine's son, Grand Duke Paul, Cameron took charge of much of the planning of the palace built for Paul and his wife, the Grand Duchess Marie Feodorovna. He designed a Temple of Friendship, the Apollo Colonnade and an obelisk for the park at Pavlovsk; unfortunately, little now remains of these.

The temple of Friendship in the grounds of Pavlovsk.

The gardens of the Catherine Palace at Tsarskoe Selo, with one of a pair of pavilions built by Catherine around the lake she had had constructed when she adopted the English style of landscape gardens.

THE CLASSICAL GARDEN IN AMERICA: A LATECOMER

The United States in no time spread across a continent, with wide climatic variants from east to west, north to south. Gardens—which in any case were first and foremost intended for the production of food—were designed according to their geographical position. Any early ornamental gardens that were created originally reflected the European roots of their makers. Dutch gardens, French gardens—they could all be seen along that stretch of the Atlantic coast that was relatively densely populated. As the classical took root in architecture, so some Americans began to look at the accompanying gardens their English counterparts had created. Although they began to follow the new English style of sweeps of land with vistas and views, the idea of carefully placed symbolic buildings was not widely endorsed.

A Belgian, André Parmentier, who arrived in New York in 1824, is generally considered the first person to spread the virtues of the landscaped classical garden to the New World. But although landscaping took place on large country estates, representations of English Neoclassical gardens, with their philosophical and classical allusions, were not really designed until the beginning of the twentieth century—nearly 200 years after work first started at Stowe. Dumbarton Oaks in Washington, D.C., started in 1921 by Beatrix Farrand, combines different elements of the European classical garden, but is more a poem in praise of it, rather than an original song.

Dumbarton Oaks garden, Washington DC. An example of an early twentieth-century continuation of the Neoclassical garden tradition.

The Monopteros in the Englischer Garten in Munich. It was designed by Leo von Klenze in 1833–8 as a temple monument to the Elector Karl Theodor, who had laid out a new public park in 1789 in the style of a landscape garden.

ANGLICIZED GERMAN GARDENS

About German gardens Horace Walpole wrote: 'The little Princes of Germany who spare no profusion on their palaces and country house, are most likely to be our imitators; especially as their country and climate bears in many parts resemblance to ours.' Indeed, there was a move in Germany towards the end of the eighteenth century to emulate the landscape gardens of England, with gardens like that at Wörlitz, the home of Prince Franz of Anhault-Dessau, which encompassed water, temples, vistas and an undulating park. A large garden, it was begun in 1765, but not finished until 1817. Prince Franz was much involved with the design, which was inspired by the gardens at Stowe, Stourhead, Claremont and The Leasowes.

Generally, the new natural garden in Europe held sway throughout the remainder of the eighteenth century, and on into the nineteenth, until the emergence of the very different Victorian garden.

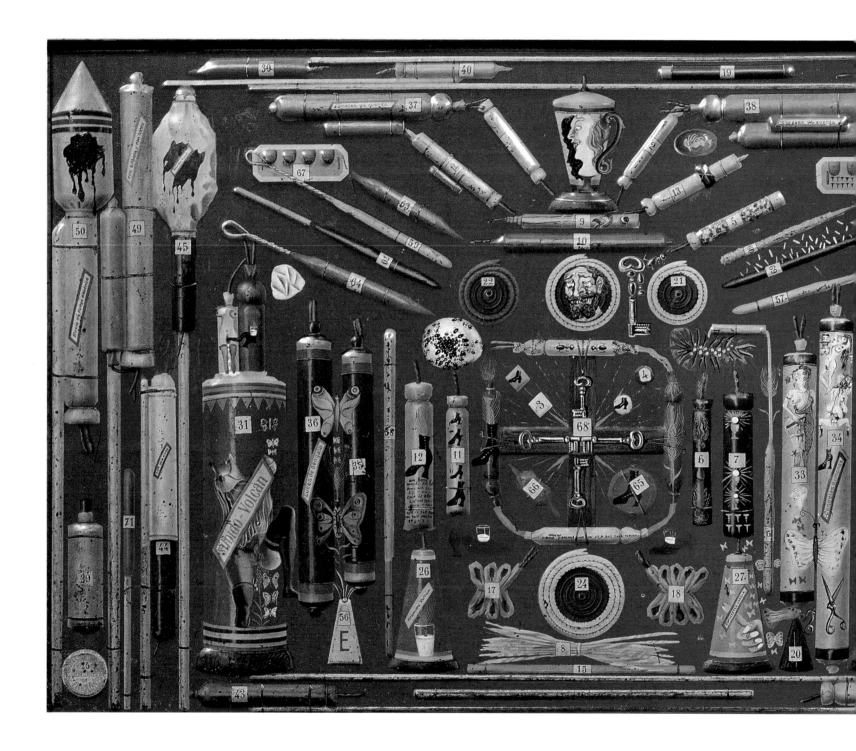

Fireworks *by Salvador Dali. The decorative contents are both a parody of the motifs so often used in Neoclassical art, and an appreciation of the ordered symmetry of such designs.*

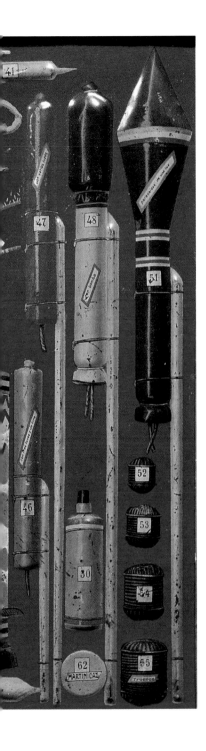

VIII

THE NEOCLASSICAL HERITAGE

I T WAS INEVITABLE THAT the comparative purity and inventiveness of Neoclassical architecture would eventually weaken. By the middle of the nineteenth century, the Arcadian vision had become, for the most part, an exercise in archaeological architecture—or excavation through architecture. The Neoclassical was an accepted style, part of the establishment, and it was time, yet again, for a reaction. Radical design movements like those led by A. W. N. Pugin, William Morris and William Burges challenged the classical ideal. As well, there were other architects, historians, designers and theorists who championed seemingly every architectural style ever developed, encompassing buildings that ranged from Tudor piles to fairy castles, most of them loosely based on some sort of connection with a real or imagined past.

EVER-VALID AND -SUITABLE CLASSICISM

But in the 1800s and beyond—even up to today—the ideas behind classical architecture remained as valid as they had always been. Based on firm mathematical and artistic principles, with fixed disciplines of proportion and space, classical lines were still suitable for both domestic and public buildings and, increasingly, monumental architecture.

Monuments and memorials have always followed the classical mode. Napoleon used classical precedent to emphasize his own military might and victories, as exemplified by the copy of Trajan's Column that was reincarnated by Gondoin as the Colonne de la Grande Armée in the Place Vendôme, cast from the bronze of captured cannons, and the straight-forward lift of the Arc de Triomphe, borrowed from Roman triumphal arches. There were American edifices, too, such as the Lincoln and Jefferson memorials, both in Washington, D.C., which were built as emblems of a classical past.

AMERICAN NEOCLASSICISM CONTINUES

Nascent countries born out of revolutions like the United States found the classical expression right for their times. Throughout the nineteenth century, significant new buildings such as State Capitols were more often than not built in the classical style, with the emphasis firmly on the Greek Revival.

The Parthenon and the Erechtheum both found themselves, far from the Acropolis, inspiring buildings in South Carolina, Pennsylvania, New York and elsewhere. Towards the end of the 1800s, a new form of classical revival, inspirational rather than derivative, produced buildings like the low-domed, Ionian-columned Low Library at New York's Columbia University, and the famous Villard Houses on Manhattan's Madison Avenue, both from the practice of McKim, Mead & White, which confidently took America into the new century. Neoclassicism remained a popular style for large private houses.

The Lincoln Memorial, Washington DC designed by Henry Bacon between 1915 and 1922. Although by this time architects like Frank Lloyd Wright were experimenting with shape, many public monuments were still being built true to the classical tradition.

The colonnades in Heroes' Square, Budapest, designed by Albert Schickedanz in 1896.
A late addition to the European classical repertoire, and not an entirely successful one.

THE BRUTAL NEOCLASSICISM OF TOTALITARIANISM

As the nineteenth century merged with the twentieth, classical forms lost none of their magic for those trying to impose their will upon the world. Stalin, Mussolini and Hitler were seduced by the implicit power of classical architecture, and used it to convey their ideas of revolution and grandeur. Mussolini went so far in his attempt to re-create the glory of classical Rome as to build a new Foro Italico in the city.

One of the most infamous and best documented uses of classical architecture to convey brutal might was that instigated by the architect of the Third Reich, Albert Speer. Hitler was obsessed by architecture, wanting to build with a monumentality he felt appropriate to a great empire. Speer's explanation of the thinking behind both Hitler and Mussolini's architecture, from his 1969 book, *Inside the Third Reich*, encapsulates the theory of monumental architecture:

> Naturally, a new national consciousness could not be awakened by architecture alone. But when after a long spell of inertia a sense of national grandeur was born anew, the monuments of men's ancestors were the most impressive exhortations. Today, for example, Mussolini could point to the buildings of the Roman Empire as symbolizing the heroic spirit of Rome. Thus he could fire his nation with the idea of a modern empire.

Classical references abounded in Speer's designs for the plans of the new Berlin that Hitler was so intent on creating, including a great domed assembly hall, which was to be both spiritually and actually modelled on the Roman Pantheon. The parallels were obvious, and Speer himself called the last buildings designed before the war neo-Empire, 'comparable to the style that prevailed . . . shortly before Napoleon's fall'.

Later, this early architecture of revolution and war became debased into the architecture of the institutional, representative only of a faceless centralized bureaucracy. Whether it was the dour buildings of Eastern Europe, or the fussy outline of a committee-approved Western town hall, any affinity with the majesty of classical architecture was lost, and, for a while, these unimaginative and uninspired public buildings gave classical architecture an indifferent if not a bad name.

TODAY'S GROWING INTEREST IN CLASSICISM

Our own century, however, has seen a renaissance of classical ideals. Mass communications and travel have brought the original classical designs of Ancient Greece and Rome to the attention of millions of people. This new knowledge, coupled perhaps with a reaction to some of the harsher facets of Modernist architecture, has meant that over the last fifty years there has been growing a new interest in our heritage, as well as a desire to perpetuate the beauties of classical architecture. Coupled with the realization of the necessity of preserving what remains, this new climate means that classical architects and designers are gathering a new group of admirers. In fact, classical architecture never went away. It merely became submerged beneath the noise of other, more aggressive movements. There have always been classical architects, especially in the United States and Great Britain.

LUTYENS, ERITH AND OTHER BRITONS

One of the earliest and best known twentieth-century British architects to design within the classical idiom was Edwin Lutyens (1869–1944). In many of his country houses, and several of his public buildings, he employed a style that was indebted to Arts and Crafts designs, but he did so in a classical, almost Palladian manner.

Opposite: *The Viceroy's house in New Delhi, built between 1912 and 1927 by Sir Edwin Lutyens who was, until his death in 1944, a champion of twentieth-century classicism. He had the ability, as seen here, to adapt Western classicism to Eastern culture.*

Henley Royal Regatta headquarters building by Terry Farrell, 1986. Here, one of Britain's leading contemporary architects uses pure Neoclassical elements in a playful, post-Modernist idiom.

Raymond Erith (1904–73) was a firm believer in the importance of the classical tradition, citing names like Palladio and John Soane, whose 'progressive classicism' he admired. Erith used pediments and porticoes in a restrained classical manner, typified by his buildings at Lady Margaret Hall in Oxford, including the entrance gate and Fellows' Library, and by smaller projects as diverse as his showrooms for the antiques dealers, Mallett & Son of New Bond Street, London. His pupil and later partner, Quinlan Terry, continues the tradition, as does one of the youngest of the new classical architects, Robert Adam (b. 1948), who as well as publishing a book on classical architecture, is organizing a new translation of Vitruvius. Thinking of himself as a revivalist, Robert Adam continues the tradition of classical architecture in a way that is appropriate for today, using new technology and materials where appropriate.

The Richmond Riverside Development by Quinlan Terry, 1989, who is one of Britain's leading modern classicists.

Development by Quinlan Terry in London's Soho, blending new buildings with eighteenth-century ones.

The Clore Gallery, the newest extension of the Tate Gallery in London. Designed by James Stirling, the Neoclassical elements, as so often in history, are used to connect the new acceptably with the old.

The Howard Building at Downing College, Cambridge, designed by Quinlan Terry in such a manner as to make it sympathetic with Wilkins' original building, which dates from 1800. However, the newer building has more in common with Italian Neoclassicism than the work of Wilkins, who was a Greek Revivalist.

CLASSICISM AND INTERIOR DESIGN TODAY

In the United States there have been countless architects working loosely, or more closely, within the classical tradition this century. In continuing the architecture of their own heritage, some utilize classical references where they are deemed appropriate. Others are more committed to full-blown classical ideals. Philip Johnson (b. 1906) is now a self-confessed disciple of classical ideals. Once closely associated with Modernism and the International Style, he described himself, in a piece written in 1981, as 'being brought up by Mies van der Rohe, the Schinkel worshipper, then falling under the spell of Ledoux and Gilly—I was conditioned to classicism as a boy.'

Robert Venturi (b. 1925) utilizes classicism with wit and a light touch, and over a wide range of designs. His 1979 country house, based on George Washington's home, Mount Vernon, has many classical references, but was designed and modified to be appropriate to the twentieth century. In a completely different mode his Knoll International showroom in New York interprets Robert Adam's decorated stucco ceiling in the Etruscan Room at Osterley Park on luminous plastic.

Michael Graves (b. 1934) is known today for his Post-Modern designs for everything from clocks to kettles, but is first and foremost an architect and furniture designer, one who has constantly espoused the classical in his work, and some of whose furniture places itself neatly in the continuing

The Piazza Italiana in New Orleans, designed by A. Perez and Associates and Charles Moore in 1976. Whilst hardly serious in tone, even this pastiche of classicism still works well in a public place.

Inside Michael Graves' Humana building, with Neoclassical references in the reeded columns of wood, and the sofas, also designed by Graves, complete with Empire curve.

Neoclassical tradition. He has also designed buildings that very deliberately display classical elements.

In interior design, the 1980s saw an increasing use of classical reference, in some cases so much that the finished design can founder under a sea of pastiche. But well-conceived schemes, using the timeless, internationally understood motifs of classicism—the orders, the motifs and the ornament—can add greatly to an interior, whether used in conjunction with modern or traditional furniture. There are two strands of the classical revival in recent interior design. The first is the re-creation by designers, fabric and wallpaper companies, and furniture-makers of replicas of Neoclassical designs. The second is the application of classical references and motifs, but in a modern context. Then there are those designers who

do both. In Britain, the highly respected David Mlinaric not only restores famous classical interiors for the National Trust in a sympathetic, undramatic way, but also works for private clients. Other interior designers like David Hicks have never strayed from classicism, but have always used it in a modern context, in a manner that is both workable and attractive. Younger architects, like the fortuitously named Robert Adam, follow classical style inside and out.

In the United States today, the Neoclassical—whether in the guise of Empire, Regency or Biedermeier—plays an important part in the work of many designers of interiors. These include Michael Graves and John Saladino, the latter of whom often combines the spare lines of the classical with the equally spare lines of the modern, doing so in a restrained manner

The Ionic Villa, in the Veneto, by architect Quinlan Terry. This 1990 interior by Ian Grant/Clifton Interiors recreates the mood of eighteenth-century Neoclassicism in a modern setting.

that others seem to lack.

In gardening, too, the classical ideal is still alive. Ian Hamilton Finlay, the Scottish poet and sculptor, has created a sculptural garden in the Neoclassical mode in Little Sparta, his garden in Scotland. With paths and perspectives, it leads from area to area, the spaces often marked with an inscription, poem or monument. Columns, both whole and broken, stand as signals, and they range from the Corinthian-capital variety to one newly made, taken from a design by Ledoux. The inspiration of the painter Claude is commemorated both on a bridge and in huge stones set into the hillside. Although Finlay's garden is unusual in its poetic espousal of eighteenth-century ideals, perhaps some of the new sculpture gardens created in the last twenty years, like that designed by the architect Sir

Frederick Gibberd (1908–84) at Harlow New Town (where he also designed the public gardens), are the new, accepted face of Neoclassical landscaping. Gibberd's own garden was created over several years to display his large collection of sculpture. With *allées* that lead to clearings, and walks that end in vistas, his garden is very much in the tradition of those earlier circuit gardens.

As with all important artistic movements, enthusiasm for the classical ebbs and flows. The start of this decade, the last of the twentieth century, brings a perceptible renewal of interest in the ideas and ideals behind classical design. So, quietly—against the tide of other movements—the unbroken thread of classical architecture and design continues to impress its mark on modern life.

This modern London interior is painted and decorated in the Neoclassical style by Francis Martin, and features pretty trompe l'oeil Neoclassical motifs.

U.K. SOURCES

The following specialize in supplying Neoclassical antiques or objects and designs in Neoclassical style.

ANTIQUE FURNITURE
Peter Allen Antiques, 17a Nunhead Green, London SE15.
    Tel: 071-732 1968
Bennison Ltd, 91 Pimlico Road, London SW1. Tel: 071-730 3370
F. E. and A. Briggs, 73 Ledbury Road, London W11. Tel: 071-727 0909
Rupert Cavendish, 610 King's Road, London SW6. Tel: 071-731 7041
Great Brampton House Antiques, Madley, Herefordshire.
    Tel: 0981 250244
Carlton Hobbs, 46 Pimlico Road, London SW1. Tel: 071-730 3640

ANTIQUE TEXTILES
Marilyn Garrow, 6 The Broadway, White Hart Lane, London SW13.
    Tel: 081-392 1655
Christopher Moore, The Lacey Gallery, 38 Ledbury Road, London W11.
    Tel: 071-229 9105

ARCHITECTURAL ANTIQUES
Brighton Architectural Salvage, 33–4 Gloucester Road, Brighton, East Sussex. Tel: 0273 681656
LASSCO, St Michael's Church, Mark Street, London EC2.
    Tel: 071-739 0448
Walcot Reclamation, 108 Walcot Street, Bath, Avon. Tel: 0225 444404

CARVING
Carvers and Gilders, Charterhouse Works, 9 Eltringham Street, London SW18. Tel: 081-870 7047

DECORATORS AND PAINTERS
Farlow and Boulter Studio, 22 Grand Union Centre, Ladbroke Grove, London W10. Tel: 081-969 2847

FABRICS
G. P. and J. Baker, 17 Berners Street, London W1. Tel: 071-636 8412
Rupert Cavendish Textiles, 98 Waterford Road, London SW6.
    Tel: 071-384 2642
Cole and Son, 18 Mortimer Street, London W1. Tel: 071-580 1066
Colefax and Fowler, 39 Brook Street, London W1. Tel: 071-493 2231
Gainsborough Silk Weaving Co., Alexandra Road, Chilton, Sudbury, Suffolk. Tel: 0787 72081
Hodsoll McKenzie Cloths, 52 Pimlico Road, London SW1.
    Tel: 071-730 2877
H. A. Percheron, 97 Cleveland Street, London W1. Tel: 071-580 1192
Timney Fowler, 388 King's Road, London SW3. Tel: 071-351 6562
Warner Fabrics, 7 Noel Street, London W1. Tel: 071-439 2411
Watts and Co., 7 Tufton Street, London W1. Tel: 071-222 2893

GARDEN STATUARY
Chilstone, Sprivers Estate, Horsmonden, Tonbridge, Kent. Tel: 089-272 3266
Crowther of Syon Lodge, Busch Corner, London Road, Isleworth, Middlesex. Tel: 081-560 7978

PAINTINGS AND PRINTS
Norman Blackburn, 23 Ledbury Road, London W11: Tel: 071-229 5316

PAINTS
Auro Organic Paints, White Horse House, Crown Hill, Ashdon, Saffron Walden, Essex. Tel: 0799 84888
Papers and Paints, 4 Park Walk, London SW10. Tel: 071-352 8626

PAPER TROMPE L'OEIL
Ornaments, P.O. Box 784, London SW7. Tel: 071-584 3857

PLASTERWORK
G. Jackson and Sons, Unit 19, Mitcham Industrial Estate, Streatham Road, Mitcham, Surrey. Tel: 081-648 4343

RUGS AND CARPETS
Axminster Carpets Ltd, Axminster, Devon. Tel: 0297 33533
Vigo Carpet Gallery, 6a Vigo Street, London W1. Tel: 071-439 6971

WALLPAPERS
Bauer and Ingram, 13 Crescent Place, London SW3. Tel: 071-581 9077
Cole and Co., 18 Mortimer Street, London W1. Tel: 071-580 1066
Zuber, 28 rue Zuber, 68170 Rixheim, France. Tel: 010-33-89-44-13-88
    (although French, they do supply to Britain)

GENERAL INFORMATION
Both the following organizations can help with general advice and suggestions on where to find the right experts, specialist suppliers, and craftsmen who understand the Neoclassical period.

The Georgian Group, 37 Spital Square, London E1. Tel: 071-377 1722
The Guild of Master Craftsman, Castle Place, 166 High Street, Lewes, East Sussex. Tel: 0273 478449

U.S. SOURCES

Note: Many of the furniture and fabric sources listed are open to the design trade only. Please phone for information first.

ANTIQUES

Didier Aaron, 32 East 67th Street, New York, NY 10021.
Tel: (212) 988-5248

Agostino Antiques, 808 Broadway, New York, NY 10003.
Tel: (212) 533-3355, (212) 533-5566

Yale R. Burge Antiques, 305 East 63rd Street, New York, NY 10021.
Tel: (212) 808-4005

Elizabeth R. Daniel, 2 Gooseneck Road, Chapel Hill, NC 27514.
Tel: (919) 968-3041

David Dunton Antiques, Route 132, off Route 47, Woodbury, CT 06798.Tel: (203) 263-5355

Florian Papp, 962 Madison Avenue, New York, NY 10021.
Tel: (212) 228-6770

Le Cadet De Gasgogne, Gilbert Gestas, Inc. 1015 Lexington Avenue, New York, NY 10021. Tel: (212) 744-5925

Hirschl & Adler Galleries, 21 East 70th Street, New York, NY 10021.
Tel: (212) 535-8810

Clinton R. Howell, Westchester Avenue, Scotts Corners, Pound Ridge, NY 10576. Tel: (914) 764-5168

C.M. Leonard Antiques, 1577 York Avenue, New York, NY 10028.
Tel: (212) 861-6821

H.M. Luther, 35 East 76th Street, New York, NY 10021.
Tel: (212) 439-7919

Macy's Interior Design Studio, The Corner Shop, 34th Street & Broadway, New York, NY 10001. Tel: (212) 736-5151

Malmaison Antiques, 253 East 74th Street, New York, NY 10021.
Tel: (212) 288-7569

Reymer-Jourdan Antiques, 43 East 10th Street, New York, NY 10003.
Tel: (212) 674-4470

Ritter Antik, 1166 Second Avenue, New York, NY 10021.
Tel: (212) 644-7442

Niall Smith Antiques, 344 Bleecker Street, New York, NY 10012.
Tel: (212) 255-0660

Vernay-Jussel, 625 Madison Avenue, New York, NY 10022.
Tel: (212) 308-1906

Victor Antiques, 65 Greene Street, New York, NY 10012.
Tel: (212) 941-9193

Frederick P. Victoria & Son, 154 East 55th Street, New York, NY 10022. Tel: (212) 755-2549

A La Vieille Russie, 781 Fifth Avenue, New York, NY 10022.
Tel: (212) 752-1727

Don Yarton, 922 San Pedro Avenue, San Antonio, TX 78212.
Tel: (512) 222-2820

CONTEMPORARY FURNITURE AND TEXTILES

Baker Furniture, 200 Lexington Avenue, New York, NY 10016.
Tel: (212) 779-8810

Ballard Designs, 1670 DeFoor Avenue, Atlanta, GA 30318.
Tel: (404) 351-5099

Bonaventure Furniture Industries, 894 Bloomfield Avenue, Montreal, Quebec, Canada H2V 3S6. Tel: (514) 270-7311

Brunschwig & Fils, 979 Third Avenue, New York, NY 10022.
Tel: (212) 838-7878

Buccellati, 46 East 57th Street, New York, NY 10022.
Tel: (212) 308-2900

Casa Bique, P.O. Box 788, 500 Carolina Avenue, Thomasville, NC 27360. Tel: (919) 472-7700

Casa Stradivari, 221 McKibbin Street, Brooklyn, NY 11206.
Tel: (718) 386-0048

Donghia, 979 Third Avenue, New York, NY 10022.
Tel: (212) 935-3713

Grange Furniture, 200 Lexington Avenue, New York, NY 10016.
Tel: (212) 685-9057

Greenbaum Interiors, 101 Washington Street, Paterson, NJ 07505.
Tel: (201) 279-3000, (201) 766-5000

P.E. Guerin, 23 Jane Street, New York, NY 10014.
Tel: (212) 753-7300

Henredon Furniture Company, P.O. Box 70, Morganton, NC 28655.
Tel: (704) 437-5261

Hickory Furniture Company, P.O. Box 998, Hickory, NC 28601.
el: (704) 322-8624

Jeffco, One North Broadway, White Plains, NY 10601.
el: (914) 682-0303

Lee Jofa, 979 Third Avenue, New York, NY 10022.
Tel: (212) 688-0444

George J. Kempler Furniture Company, 160 Fifth Avenue, New York, NY 10010. Tel: (212) 989-1180

Kirk-Brummel Associates, 979 Third Avenue, New York, NY 10022.
Tel: (212) 477-8590

Kohler Co., Design Center, 444 Highland Drive, Kohler, WI 53044.
Tel: (414) 457-4441

KPS, 200 Lexington Avenue, New York, NY 10016.
Tel: (212) 686-7784

Jack Lenor Larson, 232 East 59th Street, New York, NY 10022.
Tel: (212) 674-3993

Luten-Clarey-Stern, 1059 Third Avenue, New York, NY 10021.
Tel: (212) 838-6420

Martex, 1221 Sixth Avenue, New York, NY 10020. Tel: (212) 382-5185

Masterworks, P.O. Box M, Marietta, GA 30061. Tel: (404) 423-9000

Milari, 136 East 57th Street, New York, NY 10022.
Tel: (212) 319-4400

Palazzetti, 515 Madison Avenue, New York, NY 10022.
Tel: (212) 832-1199

Swid Powell Design, 213 East 49th Street, New York, NY 10017.
Tel: (212) 753-0606

Rosecore Carpet Co., 979 Third Avenue, New York, NY 10022.
Tel: (212) 421-7272

Saladino Furniture, 305 East 63rd Street, New York, NY 10021.
Tel: (212) 838-0500

Sarried, P.O. Box 3548, Airport Road, Wilson, NC 27894.
Tel: (919) 291-1414

F. Schumacher & Co., 79 Madison Avenue, New York, NY 10016.
Tel: (212) 213-8100

Smith & Watson, 305 East 63rd Street, New York, NY 10021.
Tel: (212) 355-5615

William Ellis Smith Studio, 1947 Caherenga Boulevard, Los Angeles, CA 90068. Tel: (212) 464-4644

Stark Carpet, 979 Third Avenue, New York, NY 10022.
Tel: (212) 752-9000

Steuben Glass, 715 Fifth Avenue, New York, NY 10022.
Tel: (212) 752-1441

Stroheim & Romann, 155 East 56th Street, New York, NY 10022.
Tel: (212) 691-0700

Tiffany & Co., 727 Fifth Avenue, New York, NY 10022.
Tel: (212) 755-8000

Urban Woods, 100 Water Street, Fulton Landing, Brooklyn, NY 11201.
Tel: (718) 875-9663

Sherle Wagner, 60 East 57th Street, New York, NY 10022.
Tel: (212) 758-3300

John Stewart, 979 Third Avenue, New York, NY 10022.
Tel: (212) 421-1200

Worthington Group, 652 Miami Circle, Atlanta, GA 30324.
Tel: (404) 872-1608

ARCHITECTS AND DESIGNERS

Jean Paul Beaujard, 209 East 76th Street, New York, NY 10021.
Tel: (212) 249-3790

Ward Bennett, 1 West 72nd Street, New York, NY 10023.
Tel: (212) 580-1358

Bilhuber, 19 East 65th Street, New York, NY 10021.
Tel: (212) 517-7673

Victoria Borus Designs, 111 Wooster Street, New York, NY 10012.
Tel: (212) 431-4908

Samuel Botero Assoc., 150 East 58th Street, New York, NY 10022.
Tel: (212) 935-5155

Ronald Bricke & Assoc., 333 East 69th Street, New York, NY 10021.
Tel: (212) 472-9006

Tom Britt, 15 East 63rd Street, New York, NY 10021.
Tel: (212) 753-4430

Mario Buatta, 120 East 80th Street, New York, NY 10021.
Tel: (212) 988-6811

Peter Carlson, 196 Grand Street, New York, NY 10013.
Tel: (212) 925-2173

George Constant, 425 East 63rd Street, New York, NY 10021.
Tel: (212) 751-1907

Robert Currie Assoc., 109 West 27th Street, New York, NY 10001.
Tel: (212) 206-0505

Charles Damga Interior Design, 812 Broadway, New York, NY 10003.
Tel: (212) 533-8555

Denning and Fourcade, 333 East 56th Street, New York, NY 10022.
Tel: (212) 759-1969

Michael de Santis, 431 East 9th Street, New York, NY 10003.
Tel: (212) 982-9388

Melvin Dwork, 405 East 56th Street, New York, NY 10022.
Tel: (212) 759-9330

David Easton, 323 East 58th Street, New York, NY 10022.
Tel: (212) 486-6704

Anne Eisenhower, 790 Madison Avenue, New York, NY 10021.
Tel: (212) 288-3390

Fox and Nahem Design, 69 Fifth Avenue, New York, NY 10003.
Tel: (212) 929-1485

Suzie Frankfurt Interior Designs, 279 Central Park West, New York, NY 10024. Tel: (212) 769-9394

Stanley J. Friedman, 131 Spring Street, New York, NY 10012.
Tel: (212) 431-3309

Richard Gillette, 407 Greenwich Avenue, New York, NY 10011.
Tel: (212) 226-3850

Mariette Himes Gomez, 241 East 78th Street, New York, NY 10021.
Tel: (212) 288-6856

Michael Graves, 341 Nassau Street, Princeton, NJ 08540.
Tel: (609) 924-6409

Carolyn Guttila, Box 670, Locust Valley, NY 11560.
Tel: (516) 671-9280

Anthony Hail, 1055 California Street, San Francisco, CA 94108.
Tel: (415) 928-3500

Mark Hampton, 654 Madison Avenue, New York, NY 10021.
Tel: (212) 753-4110

Robert S. Hart, 237 East 54th Street, New York, NY 10022.
Tel: (212) 223-0384

Hawkinson & Smith-Miller, Architects, 305 Canal Street, New York, NY 10013. Tel: (212) 966-3875

Hobbs Architecture Group, 110 Union Street, Seattle, WA 98101.
Tel: (206) 467-8838

William Hodgins, 232 Clarendon Street, Boston, MA 02116.
Tel: (617) 262-9538

Hutchings-Lyle, 255 East 72nd Street, New York, NY 10021.
Tel: (212) 288-2729

Irvine and Fleming, 19 East 57th Street, New York, NY 10022.
Tel: (212) 888-6000

Noel Jeffrey, 215 East 58th Street, New York, NY 10022.
Tel: (212) 935-7775

Kiser, Gutlon, Quintal, 29 East 10th Street, New York, NY 10003.
Tel: (212) 505-7880

Michael Krieger, 45–17 21st Street, Long Island City, NY 11101.
Tel: (718) 706-0077

Michael la Rocca, 150 East 58th Street, New York, NY 10155.
Tel: (212) 755-5558

David Laurance, 345 East 57th Street, New York, NY 10022.
Tel: (212) 752-1152

Lemeau and Llana, 325 Bleecker Street, New York, NY 10014.
Tel: (212) 675-5190

Robert K. Lewis, 699 Madison Avenue, New York, NY 10021.
Tel: (212) 755-1557

McMillen, 155 East 56th Street, New York, NY 10022.
Tel: (212) 753-6377

Mimi London, 8687 Melrose, Los Angeles, CA 90069.
Tel: (213) 855-2567

Stephen Mallory, 170 East 61st Street, New York, NY 10021.
Tel: (212) 826-6350

Kevin McNamara, 541 East 72nd Street, New York, NY 10021.
Tel: (212) 861-0808

Richard Meier, 136 East 57th Street, New York, NY 10022.
Tel: (212) 967-6060

Robert Metzger Interiors, 215 East 58th Street, New York, NY 10022.
Tel: (212) 371-9800

Juan Pablo Molyneux, 29 East 69th Street, New York, NY 10021.
Tel: (212) 628-0097

Juan Montoya, 299 West 12th Street, New York, NY 10011.
Tel: (212) 242-0411

John Robert Moore II, 41 East 68th Street, New York, NY 10021.
Tel: (212) 249-9370

Sandra Nunnerly, 400 East 55th Street, New York, NY 10022.
Tel: (212) 593-1497

Parish Hadley Associates, 305 East 63rd Street, New York, NY 10021.
Tel: (212) 888-7979

Bob Patino, 400 East 52nd Street, New York, NY 10022.
Tel: (212) 355-6581

Pensis-Stolz, 200 Lexington Avenue, New York, NY 10016.
Tel: (212) 686-1788

Richard L. Ridge, 903 Park Avenue, New York, NY 10021.
Tel: (212) 472-0608

John F. Saladino, 305 East 63rd Street, New York, NY 10021.
Tel: (212) 752-2440

Renny Saltzman, 815 Fifth Avenue, New York, NY 10021.
Tel: (212) 753-8861

Paul Segal, 730 Fifth Avenue, New York, NY 10019.
Tel: (212) 247-7440

Shattuck Blair Assoc., 315 West 78th Street, New York, NY 10024.
Tel: (212) 595-0203

Shelton-Mindel Assoc., 216 West 18th Street, New York, NY 10011.
Tel: (212) 243-3939

Mark Simon, Centerbrook, P.O. Box 409, Essex, CT 06426.
Tel: (203) 767-0101

Jay Spectre, 964 Third Avenue, New York, NY 10022.
Tel: (212) 758-1773

Robert A.M. Stern, 211 West 61st Street, New York, NY 10023.
Tel: (212) 246-1980

Stanley Tigerman, 444 North Wells, Chicago, IL 60610.
Tel: (312) 644-5880

Robert Venturi, Venturi, Rauch, and Scott-Brown, 4236 Main Street,
Philadelphia, PA 19127. Tel: (215) 487-0400

Vignelli Assoc. 475 Tenth Avenue, New York, NY 10018.
Tel: (212) 244-1919

SELECTED BIBLIOGRAPHY

Age of Neoclassicism, The Arts Council, London 1972

Archer, Lucy *Raymond Erith, Architect* Cygnet Press, Oxfordshire 1985

L'Art de Vivre: Decorative Arts and Design in France, 1789-1989 (various authors) Thames & Hudson, London 1990

Bazin, Germain *Paradeisos, The Art of the Garden*, Cassell, London 1990

Calloway, Stephen *Twentieth Century Decoration* Weidenfeld & Nicolson, London 1988

Beard, Geoffrey *Craftsmen and Interior Decoration in England 1660-1820* Bartholomew, Edinburgh 1981

Campbell, Colen *Vitruvius Britannicus, or the British Architect* Benjamin Blom, New York 1967

Climenson, Emily J. (ed.) *Passages from the Diaries of Mrs Philip Lybbe Powys* Longman Green, London 1899

Colburn, Henry *The Private Correspondence of Horace Walpole* London 1837

Crook, J. Mordaunt *The Dilemma of Style: Architectural Ideas from the Picturesque to the Post-Modern* John Murray, London 1987

Donovan, Frank *The Thomas Jefferson Papers*, Mead & Co., New York 1963

Edwards, Ralph, and Ramsey, L. G. G. *The Connoisseur's Complete Period Guides* The Connoisseur, London 1968

Fleming, John *Robert Adam and His Circle* John Murray, London 1962

Fleming, John, Honour, Hugh and Pevsner, Nikolaus *The Penguin Dictionary of Architecture* London 1966

Fletcher, Bannister *A History of Architecture on the Comparative Method* Batsford, London 1954

Fowler, John, and Cornforth, John *English Decoration in the Eighteenth Century*, Barrie & Jenkins, London 1974

Gere, Charlotte *Nineteenth Century Decoration: The Art of the Interior* Weidenfeld & Nicolson, London 1989

Gifford, John *William Adam, 1689—1748* Mainstream, Edinburgh 1989

Girouard, Mark *Life in the English Country House* Yale University Press, London and Yale, 1978

Goethe, J. W. *Italian Journey* trans. W. H. Auden and Elizabeth Mayer, Penguin, Harmondsworth 1970

Hadfield, Miles *A History of British Gardening* Hutchinson, London 1960

Harris, John *William Chambers, Knight of the Polar Star*

Hog, Alex *The New and Complete English Traveller: Or, A New Historical Survey and Modern Description of England and Wales* London 1790s

Hussy, Christopher *English Country Houses: Early Georgian, 1715-1760, Mid-Georgian, 1760-1800, Late Georgian, 1800-184?* Antique Collectors' Club, Woodbridge 1984

Jellicoe, Geoffrey and Susan (eds.) *The Oxford Companion to Gardens* Oxford University Press, Oxford 1986

Jervis, Simon *The Penguin Dictionary of Design and Designers* Penguin, London 1984

Letters of the Younger Pliny trans. Betty Radice, Penguin, Harmondsworth 1963

Llanover, Lady (ed.) *Autiobiography and Correspondence of Mrs Delany* London 1861–2

Loudon, J. C. *In Search of English Gardens* National Trust, London 1990

Lucie-Smith, Edward *Furniture: A Concise History* Thames & Hudson, London 1979

McCorquodale, Charles *The History of Interior Decoration* Phaidon, Oxford 1983

Metcalf, Pauline C. (ed.) *Ogden Codman and the Decoration of Houses* Boston Atheneum, Boston, Mass. 1988

Middleton, Robin, and Watkin, David, *Neoclassical and Nineteenth Century Architecture* Faber & Faber, London 1980

Morris, Christopher (ed.) *Journeys of Celia Fiennes* London 1947

Pearce, David *London's Mansions: The Palatial Houses of the Nobility* Batsford, London 1986

Pevsner, Nikolaus *An Outline of European Architecture* Allen Lane, London 1973

Praz, Mario *An Illusrtrated History of Interior Decoration: From Pompeiii to Art Nouveau* Thames & Hudson, London 1983

Pundt, Hermann G. *Schinkel's Berlin* Harvard University Press, Cambridge, Mass. 1972

Rowan, Alistair *Designs for Castles and Country Villas by Robert and James Adam* Phaidon, Oxford 1985

Ruffinière du Prey, Pierre de la *John Soane: The Making of an Architect* University of Chicago, Chicago 1982

Soane, Sir John *Lectures on Architecture* Sir John Soane's Museum, London 1929

Speer, Albert *Inside the Third Reich* Weidenfeld & Nicolson, London 1970

Stillman, Damie *English Neoclassical Architecture* Zwemmer, London 1988

Strange, Thomas Arthur *English Furniture* Studio Editions, London 1986

Summerson, John *Architecture in Britain 1530-1830* Penguin Harmondsworth 1953

Thornton, Peter *Authentic Decor: The Domestic Interior 1620-1920* Weidenfeld & Nicolson, London 1984

Toynbee, Mrs Paget (ed.) *The Letters of Horace Walpole* Walpole Society

Walpole, Horace *Anecdote of Painting, Book IV* Shakespreare Press, London 1828

Wilson, Michael I. *William Kent: Architect, Designer, Painter, Gardener* Routledge & Kegan Paul, London 1984

INDEX